ALIVE AND ACTIVE

This book is dedicated to
Dom Joseph Warrilow
(1909-1998)

Adrian Graffy

Alive and Active

THE OLD TESTAMENT BEYOND 2000

the columba press

First published in 1999 by
the columba press
55A Spruce Avenue, Stillorgan Industrial Park,
Blackrock, Co Dublin

BS1171.2
G 72
1999x

0 4244489

Cover by Bill Bolger
Origination by The Columba Press
Printed in Ireland by Colour Books Ltd, Dublin

ISBN 1 85607 253 3

Contents

Preface

'The word of God is alive and active' (Hebrews 4:12). So wrote an early Christian author on discovering that the scriptures of Judaism helped shed light on what was going on in his life. The writer of the Letter to the Hebrews made sense of life and faith by extensive use of the Old Testament. Many of the writers of the New Testament went back to these earlier writings in their attempt to make sense of life and of their experience of Jesus.

The arrival of the third millennium AD is a time of questioning. There are, as at the turn of past centuries and millennia, speculations concerning the future; there are fears and there are hopes. It is a time of asking again questions concerning the meaning of life and of reality. In such a quest, human beings do not have to start from scratch. Others have asked questions and attempted answers from the earliest days of human history, questions about God, human beings, the world, life, death, right and wrong, evil and good. At the beginning of the new millennium, the wisdom of past ages can be understood and appreciated in new ways.

This is particularly true of the writings of the Old Testament, the books of the Hebrew Bible and the other books from Judaism which Christians have treasured since the early days of Christianity. For Christians, these books have an enduring contribution to make to the search for truth and wise advice, and, with the books of the New Testament, they are considered to be inspired writings, God's word in human language. The books of the Old Testament are treasured by the Jewish people and by Christians of all denominations and they offer guidance to anyone seeking to use the wisdom of ages past. But are these ancient books still of relevance two thousand years after Christ? Can any literature, however inspired, be expected to have a perennial message? Are these words really alive and active today?

Introduction

What is the Old Testament?

No-one planned the Old Testament. It evolved over centuries. Traditions were passed on by word of mouth and in written form. Tales about the origins of the world, human beings and their experiences were passed down and developed. Stories concerning the ancestors of the Jewish people were told and re-told. Ancient epics concerning the exodus from Egypt and the journey to the land given by God were preserved and committed to writing. Some material was being written down by the time of the early kings of Judah and Israel, when court life was being established. The histories of these kings were also put in writing, and the experiences of the nation. The teaching and deeds of their prophets were preserved for future generations and added to by compilers and editors. Wise sayings and poems were gathered and compiled into collections.

As time passed, this collection of books in the Hebrew language, the emerging Hebrew Bible, was seen to comprise three major parts. The *torah*, or teaching, was revered as the five books of Moses. The *nebi'im*, or early and later prophets, include both historical and prophetic books. The *ketubim*, or writings, are made up of the remaining material. The Prologue to the book of Sirach (Ecclesiasticus), written in the 2nd century BC, shows an awareness of these three major parts: 'The law, the prophets, and other writers succeeding them have passed on to us great lessons' (Sirach, Prologue vv.1-2).

In the 3rd century BC the Jewish community in Alexandria in Egypt had set about producing a Greek translation of the Hebrew scriptures, known subsequently as the 'Septuagint'. They divided the books differently as the law, the historical books, the prophetic books and the poetical books. This division led to the common Christian way of considering the parts of the Old Testament: the Pentateuch, the historical books, the prophets and the wisdom literature. The list of books accepted at Alexandria also included books not accepted in the Hebrew Bible. These seven books, known in Catholic circles as 'deutero-canonicals', and otherwise as 'apocrypha' are: 1 and 2 Maccabees, Baruch, Tobit, Judith, Sirach (Ecclesiasticus) and Wisdom. It was this extended 'Alexandrian canon' which was adopted generally by the Christians. Their holy books, the 'New Testament', were also written in Greek.

The two 'testaments' which Christianity has always treasured are better understood as two 'covenants'. The Greek word *diatheke* means both 'testament' and 'covenant'. The old covenant or old dispensation has for Christians been followed by a new covenant founded by Jesus the Messiah. For Christians, the Old Testament looks forward to and is completed by the New. It nevertheless retains its importance as a collection of books with an enduring contribution for people of all times and places.

In order to delve deeply into these scriptures, some awareness of the problems of ancient literature is helpful. Our earliest copies of the books in the Hebrew Bible date to the time of the Essene sect. The people of this religious group lived at Qumran by the shore of the Dead Sea from the 2nd century BC until their community perished at the hands of the Romans in 70 AD. The literature of the sect and numerous copies of biblical books were discovered in caves by the Dead Sea from 1947 onwards. The Hebrew script used in those days had no indication of vowels. Signs for vowels were added in later centuries. Furthermore, ancient manuscript copies of the various books often have differing texts. It also happens that the ancient translations, such as the Greek Septuagint, give a different text. Ancient literature in ancient languages raises problems for interpretation. Sometimes the reader of the Old Testament has to be reconciled to several possible meanings for one text.

Our progress through this Old Testament will begin with the book of Genesis, as we look at the first eleven chapters, containing traditions about the beginnings, and at the stories of the patriarchs and matriarchs, the ancient ancestors of Israel. Liberation from slavery in Egypt and the traditions concerning the Sinai covenant are discovered in the other books of the Pentateuch. The story of the settlement in the land allows us to consider the role of Joshua and the judges. Saul, David, Solomon and other kings of Judah and Israel then take centre stage. Considerable attention will be given to the prophets of Israel, those found in the historical books, the major prophets and the twelve minor prophets. These are considered as the continuing history of Israel is explained to the destruction of Jerusalem and the Babylonian exile, and into post-exilic times. The psalms of Israel and the wisdom books are also explored, while the latest books of the Old Testament literature, including the books found in the Greek Bible, bring us to the threshold of the New Testament.

This journey through the Old Testament will make us aware of a developing understanding of God and God's relationship with the creation and especially with men and women. Fundamental ideas, such as the oneness and the justice of God, will reappear and evolve. A perfectly complete theology was not available to Abraham or Isaiah or any Old Testament individual. Nor is it available to us. But the progress of inspired writers in discovering more of the truth of God is apparent. Some ideas are shelved only to be rediscovered later. The travelling God of the patriarchs returns as the God of the prophet Ezekiel who accompanies the people into the Babylonian exile. Some ideas, such as the wholesale destruction of foreign nations, are quietly dropped. Other ideas, such as that of a specially chosen nation, will not go away entirely, despite the best efforts of the prophet Second Isaiah and the writer of the book of Jonah. Such refashioning of beliefs is found in the New Testament too, and in the history of Christianity. The books of the Old Testament endure as the first stage, or first stages, of the continuing Jewish-Christian journey towards the truth of God.

Chapter and verse references to biblical books show some variation between the Hebrew text and Greek and Latin versions. These differences are often reflected in English translations. Whenever different references to the same biblical verse are likely to be found in English translations, both references are given in the text of this book, the first reference always being that found in the Hebrew Bible. Psalm numbers, however, will always be those of the Hebrew Bible. Translations of all biblical texts are by the author.

CHAPTER 1

The creation of good and the emergence of evil

The first book of the Hebrew Bible is known in Judaism as *bereshith*, 'in the beginning', from its very first word. It was in the ancient Greek translation (the Septuagint, abbreviated as LXX), that the book received the name 'Genesis'. The Greek word *genesis* refers to a process of 'becoming' or 'being made'. The common focus of both Hebrew and Greek names is on how things began, and how they came to be as they are. Genesis, in chapters 1 to 11, is concerned with fundamental questions. How did the world begin? How did the human race begin? How did evil enter the world? Disasters, pain, enmity, war, how did these come about? How was it that human beings were scattered, not understanding each other? How did they learn to live in tents, to produce music, to make wine?

All peoples ask such questions. Ancient creation traditions from all over the world are known to us today. Other traditional tales concern the question of evil and the beginning of human sin, as well as the discoveries and achievements of human beings. It is not surprising therefore that the ancestors of Israel asked such questions too, and that their answers had something in common with the neighbouring peoples with whom they had contact. In the opening chapters of Genesis, where universal questions are being asked, there are indeed traces of the wisdom of other nations. But the ancestors of Israel had their own special beliefs about God and God's relationship with human beings and the creation.

Modern scholarship has revealed that many sources contributed to the material now found in the Pentateuch. The classic 'documentary hypothesis' suggests that within Genesis chapters 1-11 there is material from two such sources. The source known as 'Yahwist' is considered to have been written down about the tenth century BC at the time when the monarchy began. The source known as 'Priestly' is thought to have been committed to writing much later, in the sixth century BC. But both sources develop traditions considerably older than they are themselves.

Well before the days of the patriarchs of Israel tales concerning creation and flood were told in the ancient Near East. Tablets with copies of the ancient flood tradition date back to third millennium BC Sumer. The story of the creation of human beings to slave for the gods in the tale of 'Atrahasis' dates to the second millennium BC. The legendary ancestors of Abraham are said to originate in Mesopotamia. The earliest Hebrews, therefore, might have been familiar with such tales and adapted them. What they thus produced was narrative material which was passed on by oral tradition and which attempted to give answers to basic human questions. This is not historical narrative, but traditional tales which incorporate early Hebrew beliefs concerning God, human beings and the world. Nevertheless, an attempt was made to connect the beginnings with the history of the people of Israel, to connect the first man with Abraham. It is the 'Priestly' tradition which is more concerned with tracing the genealogical line back into the distant past. Such genealogies are a brave endeavour to connect the particular traditions of Israel with those concerning all the world.

In the opening eleven chapters of Genesis we find the ancient stories of creation, the loss of the garden of God, Cain and Abel, the flood and the tower of Babel. But there are priestly genealogies too, giving in chapter 5 a proposed line of descendants from Adam to Noah, and in chapter 11 a list of ancestors from Noah to Abraham.

The Creation

The first chapter of the Bible resounds with the statement 'In the beginning God created heaven and earth.' There are in these opening chapters of the book of Genesis two creation stories. Beginning at 1:1 and ending at 2:4a (the first half of verse 4 of chapter 2) is the creation story which describes six days of activity by God and a seventh day of rest. This account is attributed to the priestly source. It is orderly, repetitive and solemn. A second account, from the

Yahwist source, is to be found in Genesis chapter 2. It is a livelier account and focuses on man and woman. Outside the book of Genesis, Psalm 104 is another creation text. Each creation text has its own perspective, its own ideology. Clearly we are not dealing with a strict record of how creation came about but with differing celebrations of creation from various contexts.

The opening verse of Genesis 1 seems like a title. This is what is to be described in greater detail in the following verses. Genesis 2:4a is the concluding summary: 'these are the generations of heaven and earth when they were created.' It rounds off the first creation text.

The narrative of Genesis 1 does not envisage creation from nothing. This concept (referred to by theologians with the Latin phrase *creatio ex nihilo*) is found later in the Old Testament (2 Maccabees 7:28). For the priestly writer, before God intervened there was the earth, the deep and the waters (v.2). The atmosphere is dark and threatening, for there is no light, no life, no order. It is a characteristic of creation stories to describe the sad state of things before the creator intervened. Mention of 'the deep' recalls the Babylonian creation tale 'Enuma elish', in which the monster of the deep, Tiamat, battles with the creator god, Marduk. This ancient Babylonian tale is known to date back to the time of king Hammurabi in the eighteenth century BC. Christian tradition has often interpreted the final part of Genesis 1:2 as a reference to the Spirit of God on the waters, but it seems more likely that the writer is speaking here of an 'awesome wind', which completes the desperate and godless scene. The Hebrew phrase *ruah 'elohim* is open to both interpretations, as a comparison of translations demonstrates. The second verse of Genesis therefore portrays, with these images of the formless earth, the darkness over the deep and the awesome wind, the hopeless state of things before the creator intervenes.

The work of God then begins. God simply speaks and the works of creation come about. God's first words in the Hebrew Bible are 'Let there be light.' The presence of the powerful word of God will be found throughout the Old Testament. Eight works of creation are presented through the period of six days. Heavy phrases are repeated as the organisation of the world as we know it is established. The goodness of creation is stressed throughout: 'and God saw that it was good.' For the moment the question of evil is put to one side. But the darkness and the threatening waters are not destroyed. They are simply controlled by God's command (1:4, 7, 9). The waters will break free and almost destroy the earth in the story of the flood (Genesis 7:11).

Plant life is seen to grow out of the earth in its various forms at the command of God (1:11). The earth also brings forth the various categories of land animal (1:24). God makes the sun and the moon, which are creatures and not gods (1:16). God creates the sea creatures and birds (1:21). But the climax of creation is the second act of the sixth day. An explicit proposition, 'Let us make man', precedes this final deed (1:26). There is a suggestion here of God deciding with the assistance of others to proceed with the creation of man. Is there a hint here of polytheistic accounts of gods deciding to make human beings? In the Babylonian story of 'Atrahasis' the gods deliberate concerning the creation of human beings when the lesser gods refuse to work.

Human beings are made in the 'image and likeness' of God. Theologians have debated the sense of this statement and considered the special relationship of God with human beings. Ancient creation tales suggest that the more primitive sense of this passage concerns God's likeness as a model for the shaping of human beings. In the epic of Gilgamesh, which like 'Enuma elish' dates back to the early second millennium BC and is known principally for its story of the flood, the wild man Enkidu is made in the image of the god Anu. The creator god in the island of Nias in Sumatra is said to have copied his own image reflected in a pool when he created men and women. Such a primitive concept is the first stage for a developing understanding of the status of human beings in relation to God. New understandings were derived from this biblical text through the centuries.

Man and woman are created together in equality (1:27). They are both commanded to increase and fill the earth. They are both told to rule over the earth (1:28). The concepts of the equality of the sexes and of human responsibility for the environment are huge issues arising from this narrative and of crucial relevance today. In so many societies women continue to be treated as lesser creatures to men. In so many societies different social groups are oppressed and marginalised. In so much of the world the environment is not cared for, and often it is pillaged and devastated for profit, leaving it unproductive for future generations. The text of Genesis tells us that human beings have a legitimate dominion over the creation, but that they are also part of creation. The priestly writer also considers it God's original purpose that both human beings and animals should eat only plant food (1:29). Permission to eat flesh will come at the end of the flood story (Genesis 9:3), and should perhaps be seen as one of the consequences of the spread of evil and sin through the world. For the moment though God judges the creation 'very good' (1:31).

The priestly writer has constructed his account in such a way that people learn about the sacred nature of the sabbath rest. For six days God worked, and on the seventh day God rested. God's rest is a model for human rest (2:2). Another theme of contemporary relevance emerges from the first creation story of the book of Genesis. Human beings legitimately expect time for rest and leisure. Such time is understood in this story to be part of the essence of the created order. Such time for rest and leisure is denied to so many peoples of the world, to some by their need to struggle for survival and to others by the excessive drive for profit of their employers. The creation story of Genesis 1 suggests better ways.

Another story of creation
The second creation story is attributed to the Yahwist source, commonly abbreviated as J, since the term was first coined in German as *Jahwist*. In fact this J section continues from 2:4b (the second half of verse 4 of chapter 2) until the end of chapter 3. These two chapters contain two ancient tales: a story of the creation in chapter 2, which focuses on the man and the woman, and a story of the expulsion of the man and the woman from the garden due to their disobedience in chapter 3. We can speculate about how these two tales

came to be joined. Did they once exist separately in the oral tradition? The two tales are now intertwined. Verses 16-17 of chapter 2 seem to belong with the story of the sin, since they contain the command of God which is about to be disobeyed. One might also consider whether the reference to two specific trees in verse 9 belongs more with the sin story than with the creation story. And why does verse 15 repeat that the man was placed in the garden, when verse 8 has already stated this? Does it too belong with the sin story?

As the creation story begins, the personal name of God, Yahweh, is used for the first time. It is this use of the name Yahweh from the beginning that characterises the Yahwist source. Just as God created heaven and earth in Genesis 1, Yahweh is seen as making earth and heaven in Genesis 2. To some extent then these two chapters are parallel. As with the priestly writer's creation story in Genesis 1, so too here the writer begins by describing the inadequate state of things before God began the work of creation. There was no bush, no wild plant, no rain, no man (2:5). It is extraordinary that creation stories through the ages and across the world begin in this way. The traditional Mayan history, the 'Popol Vuh' (Book of the Community), reads: 'there was no man, no animal, birds, fishes, crabs, trees, stones, caves, ravines, grasses, nor forests; there was only the sky.'

As in Genesis 1, God intervenes, but the first deed of Yahweh is not to create light, but to make man. In this account God forms the man from the dust of the earth and breathes into him the breath of life. The creature has no name. He is *ha'adam*, 'the man', made of clay, which is in Hebrew *'adamah*. Yahweh behaves like a potter, moulding and shaping the clay. The Babylonian story of 'Atrahasis' tells of the moulding of humans to slave for the gods. In the book of Genesis the fashioned clay is brought alive by the breath of life breathed into the nostrils by Yahweh. The man becomes a living being, *nephesh* in Hebrew (2:7). Human beings are seen as matter brought alive by the breath of God. The matter and the breath together make the *nephesh*, the living being, the person. The essential parts of the human person are the body and the breath. Awareness of the breath leaving people as they died must have led to this view of the human person. The person is the work of God both in the body and in its life. The psalmist in the creation psalm understands the breath as 'spirit' and says: 'you take back their spirit, they die' (Psalm 104:29). The animals which die in the flood lose the breath of life (Genesis 7:22). The Yahwist makes clear God's care for both the body and the spirit. There have been times both in religion and in society when regard for one or the other has been inadequate. This Genesis text shows that each individual is right to seek a balanced concern for the bodily and spiritual features of the person.

The man whom God has made is to live and work in a garden 'in Eden, which is in the east' (2:8). The man is given responsibility for the environment. The garden is provided by God, and it is used by God too (3:8). The trees of the garden provide food. Two specific trees are named (2:9), but it is the second, the tree of the knowledge of good and evil, which is to be crucially involved in the story of sin. A command is given which prohibits eating from this tree (2:17). For a moment we are in the story of sin and punishment which continues in chapter 3. The work of the man in the garden is not seen as a punishment. Man is to care for creation (2:15), as was stated more deliberately in the priestly story of creation (1:26).

The story of the creation of man continues in 2:18. The man needs a companion and helper. A primitive picture of God appears as God makes several unsuccessful attempts to satisfy the man's need. The creation of the woman from the rib of the man solves the problem (2:21). This image expresses how the man and woman are intimately related. But this creation story perhaps betrays at this point a less certain view of the equality of man and woman. What is made clear is that companionship for human beings is best sought from human beings. The man rejoices in the creation of the woman. His joy is expressed poetically in 2:23. She is called 'ishshah, 'woman', for she was taken from 'ish, man. While the Hebrew word 'ish generally refers to a specific individual, the word 'adam can have the more general sense of mankind too. The intimate relationship of man and woman finds expression in many ancient tales from all over the world. An Eskimo tale suggests woman was made from the thumb of a man.

An editor of this creation story sees the creation of the man and the woman just narrated as a justification of the stable bond of marriage between man and wife (2:24). And the final verse of chapter 2 speaks of the lack of shame felt by the man and woman in their nakedness. The shame of nudity is considered a consequence of sin. The Yahwistic creation story gives greater stress to God's care in creating the man and in providing for him, and it emphasises the intimate bond between a man and a woman.

The story of the sin of the man and woman takes over in chapter 3. The prohibition against eating from the tree and the reference to the couple's nakedness have prepared the way for this momentous story. The harmony and peace of the garden and the God-given happiness of the man and the woman are about to be shattered.

The loss of the garden of God

From reading the first two chapters of the book of Genesis it has become plain that we are dealing not with historical material but with traditional tales which provided answers to the fundamental questions of human life. The same is obviously true of chapter 3, for here the narrative focuses on the entry of evil, sin and pain into the peaceful world which God had established.

The chapter starts with the statement: 'the snake was the most cunning of all the wild animals Yahweh God had made.' One can imagine such an opening line claiming people's attention as the story was recited. Why this focus on an animal, and on such an unpleasant animal? And an animal that talks! As in ancient fables (those of the Greek Aesop, for example) this animal has the gift of speech. Only in the story of the prophet Balaam in the book of Numbers (22:28-30) do we read such a thing in the rest of the Old Testament. God gives Balaam's donkey the power of speech to deliver God's warning to Balaam.

The storyteller here has a problem. How is he to introduce evil and sin into the perfect world which God has made? He does it by making an animal, the most unpleasant animal he can find, suggest evil to the woman. It is essential to note here that there is no mention in Genesis of the devil or Satan. Evil has a mysterious, unknown source which the writer cannot specifically identify. He selects the most unpleasant of creatures made by God to make the suggestion of evil. Jewish and Christian tradition will in later centuries identify the snake with Satan in another attempt to account for the origin of evil. For the writer of Genesis 3 the question of the origin of evil remains unanswered. He simply knows from his own experience that temptation and sin can appear without warning in the midst of the good world which God created.

The dialogue between the snake and the woman betrays an awareness of how temptation can gain the upper hand in a person's consciousness. The snake shows concern for the woman, but the snake is also cunning. It has the woman's interests at heart, or so it appears. It offers the woman the possibility of new knowledge and of being like a god (3:5). The 'knowledge of good and evil' sounds attractive to one who has not experienced evil. But it will bring into the experience of human beings a new dimension, the whole dimension of the 'not good'. The Hebrew concept of evil, denoted by the word *ra'*, encompasses both moral and material evil. The new knowledge brings a sting in its tail.

In the book of the prophet Ezekiel, the king of Tyre is portrayed as living in the garden of Eden. He has great wisdom, but this brings on pride and sin, and he is punished by losing his place on the mountain of God (Ezekiel 28:11-19). In the Babylonian epic of Gilgamesh the wild man Enkidu becomes wise, like a god, due to his association with a woman, but he later curses this woman since she has put him on the road to death. Too much knowledge is the downfall of human beings.

Once the snake has slithered away the woman reflects and decides to claim this attractive new knowledge for herself and for her husband. She and her companion now stand in opposition to God. The eating of the forbidden fruit symbolises their stance of disobedience to God's command. Just as the serpent had said, a new awareness dawns, but it is a feeling of shame. Their nakedness becomes shameful. They can cover their nakedness, but the shame of guilt remains.

Some have suggested that this new knowledge, this experience of sin and its results, is a necessary maturing of human beings.

Human beings only know a state of things in which evil is present. We have no experience of being with God in the garden of God. We have no experience of a good world. In an effort to think positively we can refer to the sin of Eden as a happy fault (Latin *felix culpa*). It is true that sin, evil and pain have provoked human deeds of great heroism, sacrifice and self-giving love. From a Christian viewpoint they led to the redeeming death of Jesus. But they have also brought, and continue to bring, untold and unlimited horrors to the world.

As Yahweh walks in the garden, the man and woman hide (3:8). When challenged they each shift the guilt to another, the man to the woman, the woman to the snake. But they have the courage to speak the truth. They accept responsibility for their act.

Most of the rest of the chapter is concerned with the punishment of the sin. There is an extraordinary accumulation of punishments for the serpent, the woman and the man. One can ask whether this story has grown in the telling. The simple story of the man and the woman losing their place in the garden of God has, by its attachment to the story of the creation of the first man and the first woman in Genesis 2, become the story of the first sin, the sin which allowed evil and its consequences into the world. The following chapters of the book of Genesis will show how evil spreads and diversifies in the world. The world is not as God created it, says the Yahwist writer. From the beginning, and despite God's goodness, evil and pain have been present in the world.

The poetic form of God's words of punishment to the serpent, the woman and the man suggests these words have been added to the story. It seems that the punishment in the original story would have been expulsion from the garden and from the presence of God, as indeed it was for the king of Tyre in Ezekiel chapter 28.

God speaks first to the creature who suggested the sin. The snake is the only character to be cursed in this story (3:14). Its nature as a creature of the dust, which crawls on its belly, is understood as a result of its sin. The enmity between humans and snakes, their mutual loathing, is seen as a further punishment for the snake: 'it (the offspring of the woman) will crush your head, and you will snap at its heel.' (3:15) The later identification of the serpent with Satan has opened the text to a Christian interpretation. The offspring of the woman who crushes the devil's head is the Messiah for some interpreters, Mary the mother of Jesus for others. Christians have regarded verse 15 as a 'first announcement of the Gospel' (Latin *protoevangelium*). This is a spiritual sense which later revelation has suggested. As far as the literal sense is concerned, such an announcement of salvation is not present in these words of punishment. The text of Genesis refers to a continuing battle; no victory is foreseen here.

There follows the declaration of punishment for the woman (3:16). It is worth stressing at this point that this first sin is understood by the Yahwist writer as the entry of evil into the world. He now spells out some of the consequences of sin for the life of the woman, and all women. These punishments are out of proportion to the gravity of the sin. But the writer is explaining that all the evil in the world, all that is not good for humans and the whole creation, comes as a result of disobedience to God's command. The pain of childbearing is envisaged here as the worst pain a woman can bear. This physical evil is followed by the emotional pain of yearning for a husband who is abusive in return.

To punish the man God lays a curse on the earth (3:17). His whole life long he will struggle to eke out an existence from the soil. The earth will produce food for him amid brambles and thistles. This will last until his natural death. Once again we have a text which has been interpreted differently in later centuries. The literal meaning is that life-long toil is the punishment for sin. There is no presentation of death as a second element of the punishment. It is rather envisaged that mortal man's death will be the end of his pain. Later Jewish and Christian writings have however considered that death too is punishment for human beings. They were destined to be immortal until they sinned and lost their immortality. It is necessary to distinguish what seems to be the original meaning of the story from what are later theological ideas. When the book of Ecclesiasticus (25:24 /25:33) and the book of Wisdom (2:24) reflect on the origin of death, they see it as due to the devil and to sin. Paul in the Letter to the Romans (5:12 and 6:23) makes the same connection. 'The wage of sin is death,' he says. Such a thought does not seem to be in the Yahwist writer's mind.

After showing in these poetic speeches the unfortunate consequences of sin, the narrative continues with various statements concerning the man and the woman as they prepare to leave the garden. The woman is given the name 'Eve', *hawwah* in Hebrew, 'the living one' (3:20). Yahweh is presented as making clothes for them to replace the fig-leaves they had hurriedly put on when God confronted them (3:21). God arranges for the other named tree, the tree of life, to be guarded to stop them from eating the fruit of this tree and thereby becoming immortal. Fearful creatures called *kerubim* prevent any approach to the tree (3:24). This motif of a tree which gives immortality is found in the epic of Gilgamesh. Gilgamesh finds such a plant but loses it to the serpent. In 3:23 it is stated that Yahweh expelled the man and the woman from the garden. This is the punishment which is meted out in the earliest form of this tale. They lose their closeness to God. They are on their own. The story of the garden has tackled and answered the question why human beings feel so distant from God, from the source of their life and happiness. The answer lies in the mystery of evil, and in the freedom of human beings to collude with evil by their sin.

Whereas parallel tales from the cultures of the ancient near East have been discovered concerning the creation and the flood, no tale has yet been discovered about the loss of the garden of God. Some traditional African myths, however, speak of the separation of God from human beings. Either God lived on earth and fled to the sky due to the nuisance caused by human beings, or human beings were expelled from dwelling in the sky with God. In these cultures too the distance between the creator and the people is keenly felt.

Brother kills brother

A considerable amount of attention has been given to the first three chapters of the book of Genesis. These tales of the beginnings continue until the story of Abraham commences in Genesis chapter 12. The sin of Eden led to the loss of God's closeness. But the sin itself seemed insignificant. The story made clear that an attitude of defiance to God has its consequences. The story of Cain and Abel in Genesis chapter 4 shows that human beings are also capable of serious harm. Cain takes the life of his brother.

There is a certain mysteriousness about the crime. Both Cain and Abel bring their offerings to God. For an unexplained reason Cain's cereal offering is rejected while Abel's offering of the first born of his flock is accepted (4:4-5). We are not told why Cain's offering does not please God. There is a moment of suspense in which temptation appears. What is Cain going to do in the face of God's rejection? God speaks to Cain in 4:6, 'why are you angry and downcast?' Verse 7 is most difficult to interpret due to grammatical problems in the Hebrew, but it seems to speak of sin lying in wait to conquer Cain. Cain is not entirely wicked. Cain is perplexed by God's behaviour. Evil gains the upper hand, taking advantage of Cain's confusion. And the evil is serious: a human life is taken.

As in Genesis chapter 3, the confrontation between God and the sinner follows. Unlike the responses of his parents, Cain's reply is a lie: 'I do not know.' He tries to justify this with 'Am I my brother's keeper?' (4:9) Cain is cursed and banished by Yahweh. And yet he is still under God's protection for he receives a 'mark', a 'sign', so that no-one will strike him. This mark recalls the letter *tau* on the foreheads of the inhabitants of Jerusalem destined to be spared when the city is destroyed (Ezekiel 9:4). Cain, like his parents, has to leave the presence of God (4:16).

The story of Cain and Abel illustrates how vulnerable human beings are to temptation, and how seriously they can sin. A man can kill his own brother. Sin is not simply disregard for God's rules and regulations. It has a social dimension and undermines relationships between people in a disastrous way. Reflection on the crimes human beings have committed against each other in the course of history, both as individuals, groups and nations, confirms the desperate seriousness of the emergence of evil in the world. In their distance from God human beings contrive evil of a more and more devastating nature.

The Great Flood

The early chapters of the book of Genesis have expressed the belief that human beings lost their closeness to God and began to suffer due to sin. The world is changed due to their collusion with the mysterious power of evil. The story of the flood in Genesis chapters 6-9 illustrates how sinfulness can threaten the whole of creation.

Experience of flooding in the region of the rivers Tigris and Euphrates seems to have led people to ask 'why does God allow such destruction?' Ancient flood traditions, including the Genesis material, see such floods as punishment for the evil deeds of human beings. It is remarkable that there are detailed parallels between the Genesis tradition, which includes both yahwistic and priestly material, and the ancient Mesopotamian tales of 'Atrahasis' and 'Gilgamesh'. The story of the hero Atrahasis covers both the creation of human beings and the flood sent to punish them, while the epic of Gilgamesh includes the flood and the survival of the flood hero Utnapishtim in tablet XI as part of a tale primarily concerned with the quest for immortality. While in the book of Genesis Noah is saved due to his uprightness, the flood heroes in these two parallel tales, Atrahasis and Utnapishtim, are saved from the flood by a friendly god.

In the creation story in Genesis chapter 2 the Yahwist writer often portrayed God in human terms. This tradition considered it acceptable to describe God as moulding the clay to form the body of man, as breathing the breath of life into his nostrils, as walking in the garden. This same tradition now describes Yahweh's disappointment at the evil perpetrated by human beings. The thoughts of men and women planned only evil. God is pained by the evil and resolves to rid the earth of all life (6:7). But Noah wins Yahweh's favour.

The story of the flood demonstrates the spread of evil throughout the earth but also raises the question of universal punishment. Noah is saved due to his uprightness, and with him his family and representatives of all living creatures. God's anger at evil does not lead God to be unjust. Despite deep disappointment God still acknowledges the goodness of Noah. Noah is described in the priestly tradition as one who walked with God (6:9), like Enoch in Genesis 5:22-24, but the overwhelming picture is of the corruption of all the earth. The God who had seen how good the creation was now sees only evil. There is a stark contrast between Genesis 1:31 and 6:12.

God warns Noah of the imminent destruction of all living things. Noah is to build an ark, which is described as a huge rectangular box. A similar description is found in the epic of Gilgamesh, though the ark of Utnapishtim is much larger. God plans to make a covenant with Noah and those who accompany him (6:18). The God who is to destroy the wicked is yet faithful to the upright, and despite great anguish will not destroy the creation.

Noah is instructed to take two of each animal aboard the ark (6:19). There is a clear contradiction here between this verse, part of the priestly story, and 7:2, where Yahweh instructs Noah to bring seven of each clean animal and two of each unclean animal. The explanation of this contradiction lies in the yahwist tradition's report of a sacrifice of animals offered by Noah after the flood (8:20).

The flood lasts for forty days and forty nights. The priestly writer describes how the waters of the deep and the waters above the firmament invade the land (7:11). Noah and his company are safe in the ark, for Yahweh has bolted the door (7:16). The priestly writer seems to take a certain delight in the destructive power of the waters: for him the waters rise for 150 days (7:24). All life on the earth perishes.

The intertwining of the yahwist and priestly stories continues in the aftermath of the flood. The ark comes to rest in the mountainous land of Ararat. The yahwist writer records the tradition of the sending out of the birds which is found also in the epic of Gilgamesh in a somewhat different form. While Noah sends a raven, and then sends the dove three times, Utnapishtim sends three different birds. Eventually it is clear that it will be safe to disembark.

The yahwist strand of the flood story then narrates the sacrifice of clean animals and clean birds. The priestly strand does not mention sacrifice for it considers acceptable sacrifices will only begin in

conformity with the law given to Moses. The sacrifice reported by
the yahwist tradition, in which 'Yahweh smelt the pleasing scent'
(8:21), reflects the more primitive statement found in the epic of
Gilgamesh, where 'the gods gathered like flies around the one who
made the sacrifice.' Like the sacrifice of Cain and Abel, the sacrifice
of Noah is one of thanksgiving. Noah builds the first altar to
Yahweh for this purpose (8:20). Yahweh's reaction is to promise
never to curse the earth again, never again to strike down all living
things.

The conclusion of the flood story by the priestly writer includes
a blessing and a solemn covenant. The blessing on Noah and his
sons recalls the blessing in the first creation story (1:28). A new element appears, the fear and dread which the animals have of human
beings, who are allowed to eat any living thing provided it has no
life-blood in it. The harmony and invulnerability of creation is lost.
God allows creatures to put an end to life, though not the life of
human beings (9:5-6). In the course of history various theories have
sought to justify the taking of human life in self-defence and in capital punishment. In our day the threat to human life persists, from
weapons of mass destruction, from enmities among peoples, from
the enduring use of the death penalty, moves to legalise euthanasia
and the widespread acceptance of abortion. In the world order after
the flood, despite the allowance of killing animals for food, there is
a clear stipulation that the life of human beings must be inviolate,
for they are made in the image of God (9:6).

The promise given in the yahwist story becomes more solemn in
the priestly writer's account of a covenant, the solemn commitment
by God never again to devastate the earth by flood. The covenant is
with Noah and his family, but also with every living creature. The
natural phenomenon of the rainbow which appears after rain
becomes for the priestly tradition a potent expression of God's
enduring solidarity with creation (9:13). Despite anger and destructive punishment, God remains committed to the creation. In the
midst of the various threats to human life in the contemporary
world, the Jewish-Christian belief in God's constant care for the creation endures.

The Tower of Babel

The opening chapters of Genesis give most of their attention to stories of creation and tales of sin and its results. But they also consider the achievements and progress of the human race. The story of the tower of Babel in Genesis chapter 11 concerns an achievement which challenges God, and has extraordinary relevance to the present day, when people question whether there should be any limit to human ambition. Should human beings explore the farthest reaches of space? Should they manipulate human genetic material? The story of the tower of Babel suggests that excessive human striving may have evil consequences.

The book of Genesis speaks of the spreading out of people across the earth (9:19, 10:32, 11:2). This story explains language differences and disharmony among the peoples as due to excessive ambition. A similar plan to build a tower which reaches heaven is found in the Babylonian creation story, 'Enuma Elish', but here it is built by gods and for gods. The tower, or ziggurat, in this story is associated with Babylon (*babel* in Hebrew). As the tower ascends, Yahweh descends (11:5). 'Nothing they propose to do will be thwarted,' Yahweh reflects (11:6). It is enlightening to contrast this statement of Yahweh about human beings with the words of Job about God when he is confronted by God's omnipotence: 'I know that no purpose of yours will be thwarted.' (Job 42:2) The building of the tower of Babel is a claim to the prerogatives of God.

God's reaction is to introduce a major obstacle to human progress in confusing their languages. Here is the explanation of the ancestors of Israel to the confusion and misunderstanding which exists between peoples of different languages. Such difficulties are somehow related to the excessive ambition of human beings. The man and the woman were expelled from the garden due to their transgression of the limit set by God. Here, the excessive striving of human beings provokes God's punishment in the confusion and dispersion of the people of the earth. Both stories speak of necessary limits to human striving.

These opening chapters of the Old Testament have raised many issues of considerable relevance today. They have considered questions about the ancient beginnings of the world and the experiences of its peoples. God's constant care for the creation has been repeatedly affirmed, as well as the devastating effects of the presence of evil in the world. As we reach chapter 12 of the book of Genesis, the focus will no longer be universal and attention will be restricted to the traditions about the ancient ancestors of the Jewish people, Abraham and his descendants.

CHAPTER 2

Patriarchs and Matriarchs

Whereas the opening eleven chapters of the book of Genesis consider the beginnings of the world and of human beings and fundamental questions concerning all people, from Genesis chapter 12 attention is focused on the traditional ancestors of Israel. The genealogies in chapter 5 and chapter 11 did indeed trace a line from the first man, through Noah and his eldest son Shem, to Terah and his eldest son Abram. The material in Genesis 12-50 seems to belong to four generations of the same family: Abraham, Isaac, Jacob and his children. As was the case for the time before Abraham, so too here the biblical writers give a clear genealogical line for the traditions of the early semi-nomadic period. These genealogies should be treated with caution, since they are the work of priestly editors, who were anxious to provide a detailed list of the ancestors of Israel. The leaders of the various tribes of Israel may have come from different backgrounds. It is the tradition which has made them all sons of Jacob, who is also called Israel.

Nevertheless, the portrayal of Abraham and Sarah and their descendants should not be treated as completely unhistorical. Discoveries concerning life in the early centuries of the second millennium BC from such civilisations as Mari and Nuzi in Mesopotamia have suggested the authenticity of many features of the patriarchal traditions. It is above all in their recorded religious beliefs and practices that such authenticity is apparent. If, as some scholars have suggested, we owe the patriarchal traditions to a much later age, then such fictional material would certainly have reflected the religious traditions established and accepted once Israel was a settled nation. As it is, the religious beliefs and practices of the patriarchs as described in the book of Genesis have unique features. The references to the God worshipped by the patriarchs as a tribal god, the 'God of Abraham, Isaac and Jacob', and the apparent identification of God with the local gods worshipped at primitive shrines are signs of early stages in the development of Israelite religion.

The stories of patriarchs and matriarchs then contain some ancient features, but they have undergone development over many centuries. As with the material in Genesis 1-11, much of this material was recorded by writers of the yahwist and the priestly traditions. One can trace within these chapters developing ideas about God and God's relationship with the ancestors of Israel.

Abraham and Sarah

From the very start the chapters of the Abraham story (Genesis 12-25) portray a close relationship of dialogue between God and Abraham. While both Enoch and Noah have already been described as 'walking with God' (5:22, 6:9), Abraham makes his journeys in the presence of God. The tradition has it that Terah the father of Abraham had left Ur, the site of an ancient Mesopotamian civilisation not far from the Persian Gulf, to travel to Haran, another ancient site in modern Syria (11:31).

The Abraham story begins abruptly with God's command to him to move again towards a promised land. How, we can ask, does Abraham become aware of such a command? What we have here is not the record of an ancient dialogue between God and Abraham but a testimony to an ancient belief that God was with the ancestors of Israel. The belief in a God who accompanies the people is fundamental to the stories of the ancestors of Israel. The idea of God travelling recurs in the traditions of the exodus and the wandering in the wilderness, in the journey of God from the doomed temple to be with the exiled people in Babylon, and in later concepts of God walking with the people and with individuals.

As well as accompanying Abraham, God makes solemn promises to him, promises of land and of numerous descendants. The drama of the Abraham story is that of the incipient fulfilment of these promises. The first words of Yahweh to Abraham contain these promises (12:1-2) and they are frequently repeated. Another constant feature of the story of Abraham is his setting up of shrines and altars to Yahweh in various places, and his invoking the name of Yahweh. There are few details of this early form of Israelite worship. Only in the story of the sacrifice of Isaac do we hear of the offering of a ram on an altar set up by Abraham (22:13). But it is made clear that the tribal chief is also the mediator between the tribe and its god. The only priest mentioned in the stories of Abraham is the noble and enigmatic figure of Melchizedek, king of Salem, described as 'priest of the most high god' (14:18).

Abraham travels with his wife Sarah, his nephew Lot, their families, and their flocks. The separation of the families of Abraham and Lot prepares for the story of Sodom and Gomorrah, for Lot and his family will reappear in that story. Once they have separated God repeats to Abraham the solemn promise of land and descendants (13:14-17).

These promises to Abraham are restated in Genesis 15 in the first version of the making of a covenant between God and Abraham. This story is from the yahwistic tradition. It is also stated that Abraham 'put his faith in Yahweh and this was considered as righteousness' (15:6). The Hebrew word *'aman* used here suggests that by having faith a person relies on God and discovers the support of God. The acknowledgement of the presence in life of an unseen God is fundamental to faith. As this story progresses an ancient ritual of covenant is enacted. On instruction from Yahweh Abraham brings three animals and some birds (15:9-10). The animals are divided, the birds sacrificed whole. Amid an atmosphere of foreboding a fire and a flaming torch pass between the pieces of the sacrificed animals. This strange ritual is understood as God's solemn commitment to the promise. The same covenant ritual is described again in Jeremiah 34:18. This ancient story presents God as unilaterally and unconditionally restating the promises to Abraham and his tribe. Abraham is simply the receiver of the gifts of God. He does nothing to earn such gifts.

A second narrative of the making of a covenant, that of the priestly tradition, is found in Genesis 17. In this story Abraham's

name is changed and the promises are repeated. In place of his former name of Abram, meaning 'exalted father', he receives the name
Abraham, interpreted as 'father of a multitude' (17:5). For the
priestly tradition the making of the covenant between Abraham
and God is characterised by the introduction of the practice of circumcision. The story shows how the ancient and widespread rite of
male circumcision was accepted by the Israelites and given a religious meaning as the 'sign of the covenant' (17:11). In this narrative
too Sarah's name is changed from her earlier name of Sarai (17:15).
Both names imply royal status and are understood as meaning
'princess'. The receiving of a new name from God indicates for both
Abraham and Sarah a special relationship to God. Abraham is told
that it is through the barren Sarah that his line will continue, not
through Ishmael, already born to Abraham from his Egyptian
slave-girl Hagar. The covenant is marked by the physical sign of
circumcision but also characterised by the extraordinary conception of ninety year old Sarah.

A strange interlude now follows. As chapter 18 begins, Yahweh
appears accompanied by 'two men', traditionally understood as
angels. It should be noted that the Hebrew word for angel (mal'ak)
has the fundamental meaning of 'messenger'. The first act of these
'three men', once they have enjoyed Abraham's hospitality, is to
announce the pregnancy of Sarah. This is the yahwist version of the
announcement of Sarah's conception. An entertaining play on the
Hebrew word for 'laugh' (tsa'aq) is found here (18:12). Sarah is
accused of laughing at the news, and denies it. Her laughter will be
remembered in the name given to her son yits'aq (Isaac).

Yahweh and the two messengers are accompanied by Abraham
towards the city of Sodom. Chapters 18 and 19 record the story of
God's punishment on the cities of Sodom and Gomorrah. This tradition has some similarity to that of the flood. The cities are
destroyed due to the wickedness of their inhabitants. As Noah was
rescued with his family, Lot is rescued with his wife and daughters.
One might ask whether this story arose to explain destructive earth
movements on the southern shores of the Dead Sea, the traditional
site of these cities. Abraham has a conversation with Yahweh as

they approach Sodom in which the fate of any virtuous people in the cities is considered. Yahweh assures Abraham that he will refrain from destruction for the sake of even ten just people found there. The issue of the indiscriminate punishment of large groups of people is raised. This sensitivity to the justice of God is a recurring theme in the Old Testament. 'Will you destroy the upright with the guilty?' asks Abraham (18:23). The narrative does not completely answer the question. For the sake of ten virtuous men, Yahweh will not destroy the city, but for the sake of fewer?

The story of the destruction of Sodom is dramatic. The desire of the townsmen to abuse Lot's visitors and Lot's offer of his virgin daughters to these men raise serious questions of sexual morality as relevant today as in ancient times. At the end of the tale, Abraham returns to see only smoke arise where the cities had stood (19:27-28).

The final chapters of the Abraham story see the partial fulfilment of God's promises. At the birth of her son Isaac, Sarah says: 'God has indeed made me laugh.' (21:6) But the birth of Isaac leads to the dismissal of Hagar the slave girl and her son Ishmael, understood in the tradition as the ancestor of the Arabs. Through Abraham the three great monotheistic faiths of today are united. The story of God's command to sacrifice Isaac comes as a surprise and a threat to the promise. Is it, as 22:1 suggests, a testing of Abraham's faith? Is it a demonstration that God does not require human sacrifice? Does it underline that the promises of God will be fulfilled in spite of obstacles? The story seems to achieve all these aims. And Christian tradition has connected Abraham's willingness to sacrifice Isaac with the Father's gift of the Son as saviour. At the death of Sarah in Genesis 23 another feature of the promise is fulfilled, for Abraham takes possession of a small part of the land of Canaan. He buys the cave and field of Machpelah, at Hebron, as a burial plot. The faithful Abraham sees the promises of God being fulfilled, and it is through his wife Sarah that such fulfilment begins to come about. The gifts of God are to be seen in the lives and experiences of people of all times. Awareness and acknowledgement of such gifts leads to a sense of being especially chosen by God.

Rebekah and Isaac

The material considered so far in this chapter shows how despite obstacles the gifts of God are bestowed on Abraham and Sarah. For Jewish and Christian tradition Abraham and Sarah are regarded as especially blessed by God. One might wish to adopt a broader perspective and consider this ancestor and this ancestress as representing all the peoples of the earth as recipients of the fundamental gifts of God. The chosen state of Abraham and Sarah is not unique to them. In Abraham all families of the earth may recognise their blessings (12:3).

In the story of Abraham and Sarah both patriarch and matriarch had their prominence. As we consider the traditions concerning Rebekah and Isaac it is noteworthy that the actions of Rebekah are crucial in the continuing fulfilment of the promise.

While Isaac remains in the background we are introduced to Rebekah in the exceedingly long chapter 24. As Abraham grows older he is concerned that his son Isaac should not marry a local Canaanite wife but a woman from among his relations in Haran. He is anxious too that Isaac should not leave the land of promise and return to Haran. Abraham therefore sends his chief servant to bring from his homeland a wife for his son. Rebekah at her first appearance is described as 'very beautiful, a virgin' (24:16). At her meeting with the servant she is willing not only to give him a drink but also to water his camels. The marriage is arranged but Rebekah's brother and mother suggest she delays her departure for some days. At this point Rebekah herself is asked 'will you go with this man?' Her answer is 'I will go.' (24:58) A solemn blessing is bestowed on Rebekah before she leaves. The continuation of the fulfilment of the promises depends on Rebekah's good will and readiness to leave her home. As Abraham did, Rebekah journeys to an unknown land. She goes to be married to an unknown husband. At the end of the chapter Isaac marries Rebekah, and 'was consoled for the loss of his mother' (24:67). The realism of this story reflects real situations. As so often, it is the woman who is crucial to the progress of this human family. And Rebekah will continue to guide events according to the plans of God.

As in the case of Sarah, with Rebekah too there is the obstacle of sterility. At the prayer of Isaac she conceives twins. But it is Rebekah, not Isaac, who is told by Yahweh the fate of these two: 'there are two peoples in your womb ... the elder will serve the younger' (25:23). The narrative makes clear from this point that the promise lies with Jacob and not Esau. Though his father prefers Esau the hunter, Esau is shown to undervalue his status as the first born.

It is the yahwist writer who gives in chapter 27 the story of the deception worked by Rebekah on her husband to obtain the father's blessing on his younger son. It is Rebekah who is aware of God's choice of Jacob and her trick allows him and not Esau to receive the blessing given to the first born. In the yahwist's view, it is Rebekah who arranges that Jacob should flee to her brother in Haran, when Esau plots to kill Jacob in revenge. The narrative has no word of blame for Rebekah, for she was aware of God's choice and took appropriate action to ensure that choice was respected.

The portrayal of Jacob and Esau is no doubt influenced by their being remembered as founding ancestors of two nations, Israel and its hostile neighbour Edom. Nothing good can be recorded of Esau, though a certain sympathy is shown in his portrayal as he realises he has lost his birth-right. The tradition portrays Esau and his tribe as enemies of Israel. One nation is chosen, the other rejected and hated. As the Old Testament progresses the concept of a specially chosen nation will be questioned. Is not God the God of all peoples?

Jacob and his wives
The narrative of the ancestors of Israel continues to tell of God's promise. Jacob, who is to be renamed Israel, though younger than his brother Esau, is the inheritor of the promise of God already made to Abraham and to Isaac. The chapters of Genesis where Jacob is the principal figure consider his encounters with God, his growing prosperity during his twenty years with his uncle Laban, and his return to the land of Canaan.

Abraham was said to have built an altar to Yahweh in the place called Bethel, which means 'house of God' (12:8). As Jacob flees north to escape from his brother Esau, he also has an experience of God in this place. He dreams of a stairway reaching heaven, with God's messengers going up and down (28:12). This image can be understood by comparing it with the Tower of Babel and the ziggurats of Mesopotamia, by which people had sought to approach God's realm. Jacob makes no attempt to approach God, but is awe-struck by the vision and the reiteration of God's promise, which on this occasion includes God's intention to accompany Jacob on his flight to Haran (28:15). Jacob sets up a pillar to indicate that this place is a 'house of God'. It seems that traditional pagan shrines were adapted by the worshippers of Yahweh. Traditions of both Abraham and Jacob authenticate this shrine for future generations as a holy place of Yahweh. A further narrative in Genesis 35 considers Jacob's encounter with God here on his return to the land of Canaan. The God who travels with the patriarchs is also understood as particularly accessible in certain places. The messengers in 28:12 (Hebrew *mal'akim*) suggest the concern of God for contact and communication with the people.

The first of his relatives to meet Jacob on his arrival at Haran is Laban's daughter Rachel. As Abraham's servant had first met Rebekah by the well, so now Rachel meets Jacob by a well. But whereas Rebekah showed her good-will by watering that servant's camels, in this narrative it is Jacob who immediately removes the stone from the mouth of the well to water the flock Rachel has brought (29:10). The initiative taken by Rebekah at her first appearance was in keeping with her prominent role in the family story. Here the willingness of Jacob to assist Rachel prepares us for his readiness to work long years to have her as his wife. On a more intimate note Jacob embraces Rachel and weeps (29:11). The story makes clear from the start Jacob's deep attraction to his cousin Rachel.

Dealings between Jacob and his uncle Laban are not so straight-forward. It is agreed that Jacob should work for seven years for Rachel, but Laban tricks Jacob into accepting her elder sister Leah as his first wife. The theme of deceit emerges again as it did in the matter of Isaac's blessing. And yet, it is principally from the unloved

Leah that the family of Jacob is built up. The first four sons of Jacob are born of Leah, and two more later on. Rachel, for whom Jacob works for another seven years, is initially barren until she conceives and gives birth to Joseph. Other sons are born of the slave-girls of Leah and Rachel.

The narrator skilfully combines here the tale of the fulfilment of the promises with details of family life, traditional material passed down in the sagas of the ancestors. One such element is the narrative of Jacob's revenge on his uncle Laban by engineering the multiplication of black sheep and spotted goats. Finally, at God's command and with the agreement of his wives, Jacob sets out for Canaan while Laban is away shearing sheep.

It is noteworthy that at this point God is said to appear to Laban to warn him to say 'neither good nor evil' to Jacob (31:24). We are nevertheless given an account of a heated discussion between the two men. It also transpires that Rachel has stolen the household gods (31:34). The treaty reached between Jacob and Laban has the God of Abraham and the god of Nahor (grandfather of Laban) called to witness (31:53). Are these two considered identical? Or are we to understand that the narrator allows for the existence of a separate tribal god for Laban? Whatever the answer to these questions the tradition is clear on the identity of the God of Abraham, Isaac and Jacob. These ancestors of Israel worship one god, the God of the fathers, but a fully developed statement of monotheism, that this god is the only one who exists, is not yet to be found.

Jacob's most mysterious encounter with God takes place by the Jabbok which flows from east to west into the Jordan. The text states that 'someone wrestled with him till dawn' (32:26/32:25). Jacob's hip is dislocated but he still forces the stranger to remain and seeks a blessing from him. He obtains a blessing, and he is given the new name 'Israel', which is explained by the fact that Jacob 'has striven' (Hebrew *sarah*) against God and man (32:29/32:28). This obviously primitive story has captured the imagination of Jews and Christians. It speaks of the struggle of the life of faith and of the expectations that the believer may have of God.

Jacob shrewdly sends gifts to Esau before he meets him himself.

The brothers are reconciled but go their separate ways. Jacob then buys land from the Canaanites at Shechem on which he erects his tent and sets up a shrine to 'El, God of Israel' (33:19-20). A further encounter with God is narrated in Genesis 35 when Jacob comes again to Bethel. The foreign idols they have brought from Haran are destroyed and an altar is established at Bethel. Once more God reiterates the promises to Jacob. Thus the journey of Jacob to Haran and back is completed. His dream of the stairway marked the beginning of the journey. This encounter with God concludes it. Soon after this Rachel dies in giving birth to Jacob's youngest son, Benjamin, on the way to Bethlehem (35:18-19).

The story of the life of Jacob is not yet complete, but what remains will be told as part of the story of Joseph. In the multiple traditions recorded in these chapters of Genesis the promises made to Abraham, Isaac and Jacob are being fulfilled. Above all, Jacob has numerous descendants who will be considered the ancestors of the traditional twelve tribes of Israel. They are present in the land though they possess little of it. In the story of Joseph they are to lose the land and their very survival will be at stake. The protection of God is not always apparent. The Genesis stories show that it is there in spite of appearances.

The story of Joseph

As the promises to the ancestors of descendants and land appear to move to fulfilment, the scene in the final chapters of the book of Genesis shifts to the land of Egypt. The passage of nomadic peoples from the land of Canaan to Egypt in time of famine has already been suggested by Abraham's journey to Egypt in Genesis 12. Evidence for the reception of peoples in Egypt is found in a papyrus dating to the thirteenth century BC. Shepherd tribes of Edom, the traditional land of Esau, are reported to have been allowed across the border into Egypt due to famine. It is known too that in earlier centuries Egypt had been ruled by Semitic pharaohs known as Hyksos. The story of the rise of Joseph to a powerful position in Egypt has a certain historical plausibility.

Family tensions have been described in the rivalry between Sarah and Hagar and in the favouritism of Rebekah for her younger son Jacob. The story of Joseph tells how God brings good out of the rivalry between brothers. At the very start of the story we are told that the rivalry is fuelled by Jacob himself, for 'Israel loved Joseph more than all his other sons.' (37:3) As Rebekah's preference for Jacob led to God's promise being fulfilled, so Jacob's predilection for Joseph also serves God's purposes. The stories of the ancestors speak of a God whose providence is worked out in collusion with human frailty.

Joseph has a talent for dreaming and for interpreting the dreams of others. He is bold enough to tell his dreams of his own pre-eminence to his brothers and his father. It is primarily because they see him as 'that master of dreams' (37:19) that the brothers plot against him. Signs of two separate traditions here are seen in the interventions of both Reuben and Judah to defend Joseph, but he is nevertheless sold into slavery in Egypt.

In the first stage of his time in Egypt, his service in the house of Potiphar, the writer repeatedly states that Yahweh was with Joseph (39:2, 3, 5). And this presence is again affirmed when Joseph is imprisoned due to the unsuccessful seduction and false denunciation of Joseph by Potiphar's wife (39:21, 23). This dreamer can also interpret the dreams of others, and due to the demonstration of such skill Joseph is freed from prison and becomes Pharaoh's chancellor. As will happen again in the book of Daniel, a pagan ruler recognises the God-given gifts of a Jewish exile in a pagan environment and gives him responsibility in government. At this point the promise to Israel is recalled, for Joseph fathers by an Egyptian wife his two sons, Manasseh and Ephraim, destined to be leaders of two tribes of Israel (41:50-52).

The resolution of the tension between Joseph and his brothers comes, just as it eventually came in the story of Jacob and his brother Esau. But the plot here is more complex. A series of encounters take place between the unrecognised Joseph and his suppliant brothers, who have come to Egypt to beg for food in the famine that has stricken 'all the world' (41:57). On the brothers' second visit to

Egypt Joseph makes himself known to them. 'God has sent me before you to preserve your lives,' Joseph explains (45:5). God has used the evil deed of the brothers to prepare a safe reception and a life-line for the whole of Jacob's family. 'God sent me before you to assure the survival of your race on earth', he says (45:7). Even though great prominence is given in Genesis to the promise of a land for God's people, God provides above all for their survival. As the story demonstrates, the providential care of God goes with this people beyond the limits of the land of Israel. God is not restricted to the land of Canaan where they had dwelt but accompanies them wherever they go.

Once Jacob and his whole family descend into Egypt it is no longer Joseph but his father Jacob who is the focus of the story. As Jacob sets out for Egypt, the promise is reiterated by God. God promises to make the nation great, but also to bring them back (46:4). All the sons of Jacob with their wives and children accompany Jacob to Egypt. Jacob adopts Ephraim and Manasseh, the two sons of Joseph born in Egypt, as equal to his sons.

The testament of Jacob in Genesis 49 is a lengthy poem in which the later fortunes of the tribes are presented as foreseen by the patriarch. Jacob is just one of many scriptural characters whose testaments have been inserted later into their stories. Jacob addresses each of his twelve sons. It is Judah who is given pre-eminence among the sons: 'Your father's sons will do you homage.' (49:8) There is no doubt an allusion here to the kingly line of David, who was of the tribe of Judah. The ruler of the tribe of Judah, especially chosen by God, is the figure in whom later messianic hopes will be placed. It is no surprise that Christians saw these words attributed to the patriarch Jacob as an inspired ancient foretelling of the coming of the messiah. In their context here they speak of the leadership of Judah as part of the destiny of Israel. The dying patriarch has tender words for Joseph. 'Blessings of heaven above, blessings of the deep lying below, blessings of breasts and womb, blessings of your father greater than the blessings of the everlasting mountains, fruitfulness of the eternal hills, be on the head of Joseph, on the crown of the one chosen from his brothers.' (49:25-26) Similar words are attributed to Moses when he blesses the tribe of Joseph before he dies (Deuteronomy 33:13-16).

The book of Genesis draws towards its close with Jacob's death and funeral. He has given instructions to be buried in the cave of Machpelah, where Sarah and Abraham, Isaac and Rebekah, and his own wife Leah already lie. Abundant detail is given of the embalming of Jacob's body, the mourning of the Egyptians and the journey to Canaan for the burial. Some tension still exists between Joseph and his brothers so that Joseph once again explains that 'God has turned evil to good to bring about today the survival of a numerous people.' (50:20) As the book of Genesis ends the family of Jacob remains in Egypt. As his father had done, Joseph makes the sons of Israel swear to take his bones in due course to Canaan (50:25). The return to the land of promise is however not to be easily achieved.

CHAPTER 3

Liberation and Covenant

The stories of the ancestors of Israel were presented as a family history of Abraham, Isaac and Jacob. The book of Exodus by contrast begins to see the descendants of Israel as a nation, a people brought by circumstances to live in Egypt. The stories of the ancestors could not be related with any precision to a particular time in the second millennium BC. The traditions narrated in the book of Exodus likewise have no definite setting in history, but possible links with historical places and people should be explored.

The events of Egypt are centred on Moses. He it is who plays the leading role in the liberation of a number of Israelites from hard times in Egypt. He it is who seems to instigate the laying down of laws whereby the life of the nation is to be ordered. The events of liberation and covenant lie at the heart of the book of Exodus, and the remaining books of the Pentateuch, Leviticus, Numbers and Deuteronomy, provide further working out of the implications of the covenant in detailed legislation.

The events narrated from Exodus to Deuteronomy present a developing theology. God is the one who hears the people's cries of distress, and who despite obstacles achieves their liberation. God is the initiator of a covenant which lays down laws for the life of the people. It is understood that the prosperity of the people will depend on their faithful observance of the law (Deuteronomy 30:16). A new picture of God emerges, which both builds on and differs from the theology found in the stories of the ancestors.

Oppression in Egypt

There is considerable evidence for the passage of nomadic tribes from Canaan into Egypt during the second millennium BC. In the

early years of the millennium pharaoh Amenemhet I built a series
of fortifications to control the entry of such strangers into the fertile
lands of the Nile delta. The most significant impact on Egyptian history from this quarter came in the seventeenth century BC when
Semitic rulers, known as Hyksos, governed Egypt for a century. It is
tempting to relate the journeys of the patriarchs from Canaan to
Egypt to such movements of peoples, and very attractive to find
support in such events for the historicity of the Joseph story. We can
achieve no certainty in such speculation, but we can comfortably
consider the presence of large numbers of Israel's ancestors in temporary residence in Egypt to be historically plausible.

The Pentateuch on two occasions suggests that the period of
their stay in Egypt lasted about four hundred years. In Exodus
12:40, as the Israelites prepare to flee Egypt, we are told that they
had spent 430 years in Egypt. In the Abraham traditions we find
that Abraham in Genesis 15:13 is warned of four hundred years to
be spent by the Israelites as slaves. Both these periods are discon-
nected, for we have no date for the descent of Israel's ancestors into
Egypt, nor for their departure from Egypt, and the period of four
hundred years seems to represent ten generations of forty years
each.

A further suggestion concerning the date of the departure from
Egypt is found in the accounts of the reign of Solomon. In 1 Kings
6:1 it is stated that King Solomon began to build the temple 480
years after the exodus. This calculation of twelve generations also
seems like guess-work, but knowing the approximate dates of
Solomon's reign in the tenth century BC we can calculate an exodus
date of approximately 1450 BC. It has frequently been suggested,
however, that the writer of 1 Kings may simply have concocted this
first period of 480 years from the exodus to the building of the temple by Solomon. He derived it from the period between the building
of Solomon's temple and the building of the second temple after the
destruction of Solomon's temple by the Babylonians. As with the
estimates found in the Pentateuch, the date suggested here too cannot be relied upon.

Other evidence is of more help in seeking to discover a general historical context. As the book of Exodus begins, we are told that 'there arose a new king in Egypt, who did not know Joseph' (1:8). This new king no longer looked benignly on the Israelite immigrants and initiated a policy of enslavement and genocide. It is stated that the Israelites were put to work to build the store-cities of Pithom and Rameses (1:11). Certainty cannot be achieved in this matter, but this verse suggests that the oppression of the immigrants was fully in operation when the great pharaoh Rameses II had a new capital built in the delta region, to which the name of Rameses was given. Rameses was responsible for immense building programmes throughout his empire. Furthermore, contemporary Egyptian texts tell of the use of the labour of *habiru* in such works. Reference is made to the *habiru* or *apiru* in Egyptian documents over many centuries, and seems to denote groups of immigrant workers. It has frequently been suggested that the Hebrews (in Hebrew *'ibrim*) received their name from such social groups.

At this point we can take stock of what can and cannot be reasonably stated concerning the situation of Israelites in Egypt. It must be borne in mind that we are dealing here with ancient epic material in which the intervention of God to deliver his people is paramount. The presence of groups of Israelites in Egypt is historically plausible. It is also plausible that their fortunes changed during their stay in Egypt and that they were victimised by the native Egyptians. Exodus 2:23 speaks of the death of the oppressive pharaoh, which would no doubt have raised hopes of liberation. Historical evidence for Israel's presence on the world scene as a separate nation comes in the stele of the pharaoh Merneptah, the son of Rameses II, which affirms that several nations, Israel among them, were devastated during his reign. Such eulogies of pharaohs are notoriously unreliable but this first historical reference to Israel suggests the emergence of the descendants of Jacob as an ethnic group in Canaan by the end of the thirteenth century BC. It is therefore plausible to consider Rameses II as the pharaoh of the oppression and his son Merneptah as the pharaoh who allowed the Israelite settlers to leave Egypt.

What must be stressed is that the fundamental purpose of the narrative is to illustrate the intervention of God in the circumstances of the Hebrews in Egypt. The book of Genesis showed that God had provided for the survival of the ancestors by means of Joseph. The book of Exodus illustrates how God provides for the freedom of the Israelite nation by means of Moses.

The mission of Moses

Moses is the central figure in the Pentateuch from Exodus to Deuteronomy. He is the leader in the achievement of the people's liberation. He is the mediator in the making of the covenant. To establish a life story of Moses is not easy due to the large amount of traditional material which has been attached to him.

The story of the birth of Moses owes much to traditional tales of the births of great leaders. His being saved by being placed in a basket by the riverside is a motif told also of the Akkadian ruler Sargon I, who ruled Mesopotamia one thousand years earlier. The name Moses is explained in Exodus 2:10 by reference to the Hebrew word *mashah,* which means 'to draw out'. Quite apart from the unlikelihood of an Egyptian princess giving an adopted boy a Hebrew name, the name Moses is quite clearly akin to those of Egyptian rulers like Tutmosis and Rameses. The 'moses' element in all these names means 'is born'. Moses therefore has an authentically Egyptian name.

It is a matter of some surprise that the biblical account in recording Moses' interest in the plight of his fellow countrymen narrates that Moses kills an Egyptian who has struck a Hebrew (2:12). This is told quite simply to explain his flight to Midian. It seems that the Midianites, already mentioned in the story of Joseph, were a nomadic people at this time. Moses' flight to Midian may simply mean that he left Egypt and spent some time with Midianite nomads in the Sinai peninsula.

There are conflicting accounts of Moses' contacts with the Midianites. In one tradition Moses stays with Reuel, who gives Moses his daughter Zipporah in marriage (2:21). In another tradition the father-in-law is called Jethro (3:1). More important than these contradictory details is the account of the call of Moses which is reported in chapter three, the story of the burning bush. In this incident God's concern for the enslaved people and God's choice of Moses are made known.

The incident takes place at the mountain of God called Horeb, which is understood as the mountain given the name Sinai in other traditions. Moses sees a bush which appears to burn but which is not being consumed. It is sufficient to consider the image as a powerful way of speaking of God's extraordinary presence to Moses. Moses investigates the sight and is made aware of the holiness of the place. He is told to remove his sandals (3:5).

It is the dialogue between God and Moses which is more important than attempts to describe and explain what was seen by Moses. This God is 'the God of Abraham, the God of Isaac and the God of Jacob' (3:6). An immediate connection is made with the God of the ancestors, who had made promises to them. The present purpose of God is to rescue the people and restore them to the land of Canaan. 'I am sending you to pharaoh,' God says, indicating how Moses is to be involved in God's plan (3:10).

Moses' dialogue with God continues until Exodus 4:17. The text contains a series of objections which Moses makes to the task laid on him by God. The most significant of Moses' objections concerns his ignorance of the name of God. From the beginning of Genesis the tradition known as 'yahwist' has used the personal name of God, 'Yahweh', a name never pronounced by Jews and often indicated by the four consonants YHWH. The traditions found in Exodus 3 and Exodus 6 contrast with the yahwist view reported in Genesis 4:26 that people began to invoke the name of Yahweh from earliest times. For these traditions it was to Moses that the name was first revealed. Moses objects that he cannot speak to the Israelites without knowing the name of God. God's reply in 3:14 is cryptic. The words *'ehyeh 'asher 'ehyeh* may be translated 'I am who I am'. The following verses indicate that the name YHWH was understood as being related to God's answer to Moses in 3:14. In Exodus 6:2-3 the priestly tradition explains that God, who had been known to the patriarchs as El Shaddai, a name rendered by the Greek tradition as 'almighty God', is now to be known by the name of YHWH.

As Moses' conversation with God continues the only compromise God allows in insisting on Moses' fulfilment of his mission is that Moses' brother Aaron should speak for him (4:14). This prepares for the important role of Aaron in the dealings with Pharaoh and later as priest for the people. Moses obtains leave from his father-in-law to return to Egypt. An extraordinary incident then recalls Jacob's wrestling with God. It is stated in this mysterious passage that God tried to kill him, either Moses or his son (4:24). It is the action of Zipporah in circumcising her son that appeases God. Such rare incidents make us aware of the antiquity of the biblical record and of how the scriptures contain some very early notions of God.

Moses' fulfilment of God's instructions comes in the various encounters Moses and Aaron have with the pharaoh. The attempt to convince an ever more obstinate ruler is accompanied by the story of the ten plagues. God's hardening of the heart of pharaoh and the infliction of the plagues are designed to reveal the glory of the God of Israel. The nature of the ten plagues must be understood in this context. The plagues reflect natural phenomena in Egypt, but the arranging of the sequence of plagues has a theological purpose. God intervenes on behalf of the people to demonstrate the power of God. God hardens Pharaoh's heart with the deliberate intention of allowing more scope for showing God's glory. For the believer the power of God and God's profound commitment to the freedom of the people are celebrated here. Similar celebrations of God's greatness can be found in Psalm 78 (verses 43-51) and in Psalm 105 (verses 27-36), which both tell of the plagues sent on Egypt.

The liberation

The story is about to reach the narration of the tenth plague when in Exodus 12 there is a rather sudden change of genre. The narrative is interrupted as Moses is given instructions concerning the liturgical rites which are to commemorate the liberation from Egypt. It is true that the reason given to the pharaoh for Israel's departure was so that they might offer sacrifice to God in the desert (5:1), but the shift at this point from historical narrative to cultic law is still somewhat

abrupt. Exodus 12 contains laws concerning the festival of Passover
and the eating of unleavened bread. Exodus 13 will also consider
the sacrifice to God of the first born.

The feast of the Passover seems to have very ancient origins. It
probably began as a nomadic rite in which protection was sought
from God for the flocks. At a time when new animals were being
born and before moving on to new summer pastures, a special sacrifice was offered. Evidence of such rites was discovered among
nomadic peoples of the Middle East even in recent times. It is worth
considering whether the feast referred to by Moses in his dealings
with the pharaoh was in fact this ancient springtime feast. The
instructions given by God to Moses and Aaron in Exodus 12
describe a transformation of the ancient feast into a rite to seek protection from the tenth plague, the death of the first born. The instructions given here are to serve 'for all generations' (12:14). What we are
given here are the definitive biblical laws concerning the Passover.
They are inserted in the story at this point because the events com-
memorated in the annual liturgy are about to be narrated.

The observance of eating unleavened bread for seven days is
also laid down at this point. It seems most unlikely that this observance was kept by the Israelites in Egypt, particularly in the circumstances of flight from Egypt. This is more probably an agricultural
feast inherited from the people among whom the Israelites settled
in Canaan. Since it was also a springtime feast it was soon associated
with the Passover. It was given a new meaning, just as had happened with the passover feast. Eating bread which had not been
allowed to rise was explained as due to the haste of the Israelites'
departure (12:39). The sacrifice of the first born, which was possibly
long practised by nomads, likewise receives new justification here
due to the destruction of the first born of Egypt. Every first born
male, with the exception of donkeys and human beings, is to be sacrificed (13:13).

These liturgical rites have ancient origins but are given new
meaning by Israel as rituals which recall God's intervention to free
the Israelites from slavery. Christians see such a process of adapting
ancient rites to new events when Jesus uses the passover liturgy to

commemorate his death. The apostle Paul refers to the rites of unleavened bread when stressing the need for Christians to reject the 'old leaven' in their new life of sincerity and truth (1 Corinthians 5:7-8). These reinterpretations of ancient rites keep pace with a developing faith. For both Jews and Christians the celebration of God's gift of freedom to people no longer involves the sacrifice of a lamb and the sprinkling of blood. Similarly, animal sacrifice, so prominently featured in the cultic laws of the Pentateuch, is no longer considered to be what God requires.

After these liturgical rules the narrative of the departure from Egypt reaches its dramatic climax. The final plague strikes down the first born of man and beast in Egypt (12:29). Pharaoh summons Moses and Aaron by night and gives them leave to go to worship God as they have asked.

The text speaks of six hundred thousand men and their families leaving Egypt. Such a huge number would suggest that, with complete families, two million people left Egypt. Such numbers are clearly a vast exaggeration. The question of how many did actually leave Egypt cannot be answered. This is related to the question whether all the tribes spent time in Egypt, or whether the tradition has presented as national history experiences which smaller groups of the ancestors of Israel lived through. To what extent has the epic narrative enhanced the story? How many people were really involved in an escape from slavery in Egypt?

The exaggerated number is accompanied by exaggerated events. The pharaoh quickly regrets his decision to let such an important work-force leave. Pharaoh and his chariots pursue the Israelites. This is another occasion for the glory of God to be revealed (14:4). The route followed by the fleeing Israelites cannot be charted, since places referred to in the text cannot be identified. What is clear is that the story has them make their way to the east towards the area of the Bitter Lakes.

In this area the final intervention of God against the Egyptians takes place. Two strands of the story of the crossing of the 'Sea of Reeds' can be separated. In the yahwistic strand Yahweh divides the waters and dries the sea-bed for the Israelites to cross. The

Egyptian chariots and horsemen sink into the mud. In the interwoven priestly strand Moses separates the waters by stretching out his hand at God's command and the Israelites cross 'with walls of water to right and to left' (14:22). Stretching out his hand once the crossing is made Moses makes the waters return to drown the Egyptians. This dramatic climax of the story of the escape has developed from the flight of the people across the marshy area of the delta to a dry-shod procession between separated walls of water. The Hebrew text refers to *yam-suph,* 'the sea of reeds', suggesting a less dramatic escape. The parting of the seas is celebrated again in Psalm 114 (verse 3), where 'the sea fled at the sight' of Israel coming out of Egypt. The book of Wisdom, which like the Greek translation of the Hebrew Bible speaks here of the Red Sea, further dramatises the account in Wisdom 19 (verse 7). The Red Sea miraculously becomes a green plain.

This greatest act of God on their behalf is then celebrated by the people in an ancient poem, found in Exodus chapter 15. There is considerable exultation that the Egyptians have drowned in the sea. Once again we are in touch with early ideas concerning God's special choice of a people. The choice of Israel seems to exclude all others and to lead to the punishment of others whenever they oppose the progress of Israel. Such ideas will be severely challenged as biblical notions about God develop.

The next great event in the epic of Exodus is to be the Sinai covenant. Before they reach Sinai the tradition tells of God's provision for the people amid the arid conditions of the Sinai peninsula. Just as during the later wandering in the wilderness, which takes place after the stay at the mountain of God, God provides for the people's survival. Water and food are described as being provided directly by God's intervention. Once again the epic attributes to God what are natural phenomena. Manna is a substance produced by the action of insects on tamarisk bushes. Quails pause to rest in the Sinai region during migration and are easily caught for food. These are nevertheless the gifts of God for the people's survival. The narrative is also interspersed with the complaints of the people who have been so used to the comparative luxury of life in Egypt.

These complaints are a constant feature of the story of the desert wanderings of Israel. Despite the mighty liberating deeds and providential gifts of God, the people of God are not slow to complain as they journey to the mountain of God. Human beings are often known to drag their feet when God leads them on new paths.

The Sinai covenant

The next major development in the story of the book of Exodus is the arrival at the mountain of God. The Sinai events of Moses' encounters with God, the giving of the law, and the making of the covenant are central to the tradition. It has however been argued that the Sinai experience is perhaps quite a separate tradition. In certain texts of Deuteronomy, where a summary of God's deeds for Israel is given (6:21-23, 26:5-9), the making of a covenant at Sinai is not included. Yet Moses, who was the leader in the liberation, is also central to the Sinai story. As the Pentateuch now stands the people are at Sinai from Exodus chapter 19 to Numbers chapter 9. Much of the material in the intervening chapters is legislation built up over centuries, a lot of it later than the time of Moses. Could it be that the Sinai experience was not included in the historical summaries of Deuteronomy because the journey to God's mountain to worship was simply part of the exodus escape? It was after all from the start the reason given to the pharaoh for the journey into the desert. Subsequent additions to the Sinai sojourn have simply led us to look on it as a major separate entity.

The scenery in the vicinity of mount Sinai is majestic. Was it here that Moses had his initial encounter with God in the burning bush? Was it here that the fugitives from slavery in Egypt also experienced God? The tradition that *jebel musa* was the biblical mount Sinai cannot be traced earlier than the 4th century AD. Other suggestions have been made due to the description of the mountain in Exodus 19. Smoke rises from it as from a furnace and the whole mountain shakes (19:18). This may simply be a way of describing the presence of God on the mountain, but some have suggested the original Sinai might have been one of the volcanoes in nearby north-west Arabia. It seems however more plausible for the

Israelites to have made a detour to Sinai rather than into Arabia. Moses' first visit to the mountain of God occurred when he was with the Midianites who lived in the Sinai peninsula. This is a strong element in support of the same *jebel musa* as the mountain intended here too.

The narrative states that three months after leaving Egypt the Israelites reached the mountain (19:1-2). Yahweh summons Moses and gives him a message for the people. Since God has brought them out of slavery they are to be the people of God, bound to God in a covenant. The covenant will require them to behave according to certain laws. The covenants with Abraham, Isaac and Jacob presented God as making promises of land and descendants to a people who were not obliged to respond. The Sinai covenant by contrast makes demands on the people: they are God's people and must live according to God's laws.

The covenant described in Exodus has certain similarities with ancient covenants or treaties made between great kings, known as suzerains, and conquered states, who became vassals. Treaties made by the Hittites, whose empire was based in Turkey in the late second millennium BC, show how such suzerainty treaties worked. The great king lists his deeds in favour of the vassal and lays down the stipulations of the treaty which require particular behaviour from the vassal. The vassals, for instance, should be enemies to the suzerain's enemies. Such a sequence emerges in Exodus 19-20 too. The God who brought the people out of slavery requires them to live according to prescribed laws.

Moses alone is called to meet God on the mountain in dense cloud. God proclaims to him in Exodus 20 the 'ten words', the ten commandments, which have pride of place as the first laws of the covenant. They are a concise expression of God's law and are given in the form of apodictic or absolute laws: you shall, you shall not. There is however an impression when reading the text of Exodus 19-20 that the verses listing the commandments interrupt the narrative of the encounter with God. This provides further proof of the very complex nature of the compilation of laws and narrative found in this part of the book of Exodus.

A further body of ancient laws is given from 20:22 to 23:33. It has become known as the 'covenant code'. These verses seem to contain the laws of an early agricultural society, and may date to the early years of Israel settling in the land of Canaan. The laws are often casuistic: if a person does this, then this punishment is to be imposed. The laws of the covenant code have similarities both of form and of content with the famous Code of Hammurabi, the Babylonian king who ruled from 1728 to 1686 BC in Mesopotamia.

The ten words and the covenant code are the first two sections of laws given at Sinai. And yet neither seems to fit comfortably into the narrative: the ten words seem an insertion, while the covenant code gives instructions for a settled people. This leads us to ask questions about the historical core of the Sinai story. We have seen that the journey to Sinai was plausible and even to be expected, since it was the excuse given to the pharaoh for the Israelites' journey out of Egypt. Just as Moses did on his first journey to the mountain of God, the people also experience the presence of God there. Exodus 24 will describe, in a complicated text showing evidence of many contributors, the ratification of the covenant through the sacrifice of bullocks and the sprinkling of blood on the altar and on the people. But what were the laws of this covenant? The law codes developed over centuries, much as Christian moral teaching has grown over centuries in response to new situations. The covenant bound the people to walk in God's ways but the writing down and codification of the laws took centuries and was a living tradition. It seems possible that Moses simply acted as mediator between God and the people in their commitment to be God's people and walk in God's ways. The deciphering of what these ways were was the work of the people of God listening to the voice of God in the day to day circumstances of life. As they did so they attributed the new laws they codified to Moses as laws of the Sinai covenant.

The book of Exodus also contains instructions concerning the erection of a sacred tent, known also as the tabernacle, which was the place of encounter with God and which housed the ark of the covenant, the portable shrine of the presence of God. The detailed instructions concerning the building of the tabernacle and the ark

show that this legislation combines ancient elements with later
ones. By the time this material was written down the temple of
Solomon had already housed the ark. Between these instructions in
Exodus 25-31 and their implementation by Moses in Exodus 35-40
we read among other things the narrative of the worship of the
golden calf. While Moses is on the holy mountain for forty days and
forty nights the people resort to idolatry (32:1). This story is the
most significant in a series of tales of Israel's disobedience and
rebellion against God. Their apostasy makes necessary a renewal of
the covenant in Exodus 34.

Leviticus, Numbers and Deuteronomy

We have seen that the Sinai covenant is the unifying factor for the
legal material of the Pentateuch and that the narrative of the departure from Sinai does not come until Numbers chapter 10. The whole
of the book of Leviticus contains priestly laws which are presented
as given to Moses at Sinai. Detailed laws concerning different kinds
of sacrifices include the holocaust, or whole burnt offering, and the
sacrifices for sin. The instructions concerning the ordination of
priests are immediately enacted when Aaron and his sons are purified, vested and anointed with chrism. They then perform their
duty of offering sacrifice. There are rules concerning cleanliness
and the rules for the observance of the Day of Atonement. The so-
called Holiness Code in Leviticus 17-26 seems to have existed separately before its insertion in the book of Leviticus. It includes rules
for the observation of the feasts of Israel which were worked out
over many centuries. Leviticus chapter 25 contains laws about the
seventh year, when slaves were freed and debts remitted, and for
the great jubilee year, when in addition to the remission of debts
people should return to their ancestral property.

The book of Numbers combines narrative and law. The departure from Sinai (10:33) leads to more narratives concerning the people's complaints and the provision of manna and quails. After a
reconnaissance of the land of Canaan their lack of faith in God's
guidance is punished by the sentence of forty years of wandering
(14:34). The generation which left Egypt is understood as unworthy

to see the fulfilment of God's promise. Some are struck dead by God. It is difficult to be certain about the historical value of such reports. Punishment for lack of trust in God seems the main point of such traditions. The traditions of the wandering include in Numbers 22-24 the tales of Balaam, the seer summoned to curse Israel who blesses the people instead.

The final book of the Pentateuch, Deuteronomy, is set in the land of Moab, which overlooks the promised land from the region to the east of the Dead Sea. The bulk of the book is in the form of speeches of Moses. He reviews God's deeds and God's laws, even repeating the ten commandments in a somewhat different wording (Deuteronomy 5). He exhorts the people to remain faithful to their God. The so-called Deuteronomic Code in Deuteronomy 12-26 contains some very significant social laws which emphasise care for the poor, particular sensitivity to foreigners and manumission of slaves. The social laws in the covenant code in Exodus, in the holiness code in Leviticus and here in the deuteronomic code are perhaps the most enduring of the detailed legislation in the Pentateuch. These are the earliest traces of a social awareness which will find expression in the prophets of Israel, in early Christianity and in the social concern and teaching of Christians.

Towards the end of the book of Deuteronomy the final words of Moses are recorded, his great song and his blessings of the tribes (Deuteronomy 32-33). The death of Moses takes place on Mount Nebo, overlooking Jericho and the promised land. He dies as God decrees, is buried by God, and no-one finds his grave (34:6). A mysterious end for a man who was deeply aware of God's providential care for the struggling people of Israel, and of the commands of God which would lead to their prosperity. The books of the Pentateuch centred on Moses have through him revealed Israel's God as a God of freedom, who provides for the liberation of his people, and a God who instructs the people in the ways of goodness and life. It would take some time before the realisation dawned that this is the God of all people, the God who desires the freedom of all peoples, and who offers the ways of goodness and life to all.

CHAPTER 4

Joshua and the Judges

The Pentateuch reached its conclusion with the death of Moses on mount Nebo, and the Israelites in the plains of Moab on the eastern side of the Dead Sea. The next stages of the story of Israel concern the entry into the land of Canaan. The Pentateuch being completed, we reach now the first of the books known by Christians as 'historical books'. The six books of Joshua, Judges, 1 and 2 Samuel, and 1 and 2 Kings are known by scholars as the 'deuteronomistic history' due to a certain affinity between them and the book of Deuteronomy. The book of Joshua and the book of Judges both consider the settlement of Israel in the land of Canaan, but from different perspectives.

The book of Joshua describes the entry of the Israelites under the leadership of Joshua and his subsequent military campaigns to gain control of the whole of Canaan. Joshua takes the central towns of Jericho and Ai, sweeps south to devastate a series of towns including Lachish and Hebron, and finally invades the north, capturing Hazor. All the Israelites cross the Jordan (3:1), and they all take part in the conquest of the land. Joshua chapter 12 gives a list of thirty-one kings conquered by Joshua and the Israelites. The second part of the book of Joshua, from chapter 13 to 21, tells how the land is distributed among the tribes of Israel. It is emphasised that Yahweh fulfils faithfully and completely the promise made to the ancestors: all the land becomes their possession (21:43-45).

The book of Judges gives a rather different picture and makes clear in its opening chapter that at the death of Joshua the individual tribes still have to conquer the land allotted to them (Judges 1:1-2). Cities such as Hebron and Debir, where the local inhabitants were supposedly wiped out by Joshua, still remain to be conquered.

The book of Judges also shows that different peoples inhabiting the land are still quite strong enough to resist the advance of Israel. Indeed, the editors of Judges present such attacks by local peoples as brought about by Yahweh in order to punish the Israelites whenever they turn away from the worship of Yahweh (2:14). The typical sin of Israel is, as it was in the desert, that of worshipping other gods. We encounter here the local deities, the male gods known as 'baals' and the females known as 'astartes'. The history of Israel from this point will be constantly threatened by apostasy to local gods. The 'judges' are raised up by Yahweh principally to lead a counter-attack against the enemy once punishment has been inflicted on Israel. Some do indeed 'judge' the people, as is stated of Deborah in 4:4-5. But the term 'judge' comes to be used of the leaders summoned by Yahweh to deliver the people.

While the book of Joshua describes a conquest assisted by Yahweh in which Israel conquered all and exterminated whole cities, the book of Judges reports a partial and gradual take-over of certain parts of Canaan. In both scenarios it is Yahweh who assists the Israelites to take possession of the land promised to the ancestors.

Joshua's mission begins

The book of Joshua begins with words of Yahweh to Joshua. The promise of land made to the ancestors and to Moses is restated. Joshua is encouraged in his task of leadership. We find here an exhortation typical of the book of Deuteronomy. Fidelity to the law of God will lead to prosperity. Infidelity will lead to disaster. The words of Yahweh reflect such advice. In fact traces of what scholars call 'deuteronomistic editing' are found throughout the historical books of Joshua, Judges, 1 and 2 Samuel, and 1 and 2 Kings. The advice given to Joshua (1:6-9) is remarkably similar to words addressed by the dying David to his son Solomon (1 Kings 2:1-4).

Before entering the land Joshua sends spies to Jericho. The harlot Rahab gives them protection when it becomes known to the king of Jericho that some Israelites have entered the country to spy out the land. It is at this point that we read the first acknowledgement by the local inhabitants that God is with Israel. Rahab affirms that she knows that Yahweh has given the Israelites the land. She knows too that Yahweh dried up the Sea of Reeds before them and how Israel was victorious over the kings who stood in their way (2:9-10). The people of Gibeon will claim similar knowledge of Israel's exploits when later in the book they come to forge an alliance with the Israelites (9:9-10). It is suggested in such texts that God-fearing folk will not stand in the way of the progress of Israel, the people of God. Rahab, who protected the spies and ensured their escape, is spared with her household when Jericho falls.

The crossing of the river Jordan in Joshua chapter 3 not only marks the entry into the land of promise, but also is an opportunity for the glory of God to be revealed and for Joshua's place as worthy successor of Moses to be demonstrated to the people. The priests carry the ark of the covenant to the river and the waters cease flowing and reveal dry ground for the crossing of the Israelites. As with the crossing of the Sea of Reeds God is presented here as disrupting the normal course of nature. The ark carried by the priests stays in mid-river until all have crossed. Twelve stones are gathered from the river to be a memorial of the event, just as the passover feast and unleavened bread were for the crossing of the Sea of Reeds. An explicit connection between exodus and entry into the land is made by Joshua in 4:23. The same link is celebrated in Psalm 114, when it proclaims 'the sea fled at the sight, the Jordan stopped its course' (verse 3).

The twelve stones, one for each tribe, seem to have been set up at Gilgal (4:20), though another less plausible tradition states that they were erected in the river itself (4:9). At Gilgal all the male Israelites born in the wilderness are circumcised. What was in the stories of Abraham the sign of the covenant is practised here as God's promise of land begins to be fulfilled. At Gilgal the passover is celebrated and the Israelites eat from the produce of the land.

This is the beginning of Joshua's achievement, the first stage of the settlement in the land of Canaan. These chapters have an underlying connection with the traditions of the Pentateuch. Occupation of the land is understood as a gift of God and the fulfilment of the promise. The rituals of circumcision and passover celebrate the people's continuing adherence to the covenant God who brought them to the land of promise. God's special choice of Israel is celebrated.

The conquest of the land

Despite some limited hostilities between Israelites and local peoples during the wandering in the wilderness Israel's progress so far has been a peaceful affair. The story is soon to change as Joshua and the Israelites begin conquering fortified cities in the land. These battles are understood as fought at Yahweh's command and with Yahweh's assistance. There are ideas of God here which later Jewish and Christian tradition challenged. The command known as the ban (*herem* in Hebrew), the decree from God of total destruction of all living creatures in a particular locality, conflicts with later ideas of God's care for all people. God's command to execute such destruction is found in the book of Joshua in 6:17 in reference to Jericho. The notion has rightly been rejected as an unacceptable view of God.

We have here the clearest example of an idea of God which needed correction. Israel's later openness to other people and acceptance of God's concern for them, as found in the book of Jonah and elsewhere, shows such early notions to be inadequate. For Christians such ideas are clearly at variance with the teaching of Jesus. Such texts in the book of Joshua have been used to justify oppression of various peoples. It is extremely important to see such ideas as only one step in developing ideas of God.

Jericho is the first city to be attacked by Joshua. The story of the collapse of its walls in Joshua chapter 6 is complex due to different strands of tradition. The presentation portrays a liturgical procession of priests with the ark of God and the shouts of the people finally leading to the collapse of the walls. Once again here God is seen to intervene mightily in favour of the Israelites. The ban is put into practice, though Rahab's household is spared, and a violator of the ban is punished by stoning. The ban is also enforced against Ai in chapter 8.

Archaeological excavations in different ancient sites have revealed several levels of occupation and some evidence of destruction of earlier stages of certain towns. Jericho has been repeatedly investigated but no evidence of violent destruction at the supposed time of Joshua's campaigns has been found. Similarly, no evidence of the burning of Ai reported in Joshua chapter 8 has been uncovered there. Although a complete picture of the history of a town is difficult to compile from archaeological evidence alone, it seems that some of the material in the conquest stories may not be based on the historical achievements of Joshua. The tradition of a warrior God leading people in conquest of the land may owe more to a certain notion of God than to historical reality. Ruined cities became the targets for such stories.

A dramatic intervention of God is reported in Joshua's battle with his allies the Gibeonites against a coalition of five kings from the south of Canaan. Not only does Yahweh, now portrayed as fighting for the Israelites, hurl hailstones from heaven but it is also arranged that the sun should stand still to extend the daylight hours in order to permit complete slaughter of the enemy (10:10-15). This text achieved some notoriety due to the dispute between the Catholic Church and Galileo. Such texts were used to prove that Galileo was wrong in maintaining that the sun did not move. Similar use of biblical texts to affirm scientific truths has since been understood to be inappropriate. We are not dealing with scientific statements here. This is a traditional story of a warring Yahweh who goes to the extreme of stopping the sun to enhance the people's victory. The tradition of God's warlike intervention in defence of the people, seen so significantly in the crossing of the Sea of Reeds, reaches another high point here. The conquest also includes an invasion of the north, when Hazor is another victim of the ban (11:10-11). Excavations at this site suggest a violent overthrow of this city at about the time of Joshua's arrival.

We can conclude that there may have been some conquest of towns by a group of Israelites under Joshua, but the most significant feature of the story of the conquest is that of the warrior Yahweh ensuring the triumph of Israel. Awareness of God's gifts of life and land in their history has been translated into an exaggerated epic of the wars Yahweh fought at Israel's side.

A final achievement of Joshua claimed in the book is the setting up of a federation of tribes. Before Joshua dies it is recalled that he gathered the tribes together at Shechem. Joshua retells the story of the ancestors, the exodus and the conquest of the land. He then urges the tribes to make a commitment to the service of Yahweh (24:14-15). It is considered plausible that some of the tribes envisaged here may have joined the people who had entered Canaan with Joshua. We have already raised the question in connection with the departure from Egypt whether some of Israel's ancestors remained in the land of Canaan and did not experience the escape from Egypt.

The people agree to worship Yahweh. Commemoration of these events is added to a book of law, and a monument is set up to recall this renewal of the covenant (24:25-26). Some have seen this as the birth of the nation of Israel. Ancient tribes come together to form a federation. Others see even this as an attempt to answer unanswerable questions, another strand in the legends of Israel's origins. The federation is based on a common faith and a common acceptance of a body of laws, perhaps the ten words or some elements of the covenant code committed to writing in the book of Exodus. This unity of the tribes suggests how disparate human groups can unite around common ideals. In our day human beings still find it difficult to choose to come together on the basis of shared faith and shared values, and often find themselves moving away from each other due to overemphasis of ethnic and other differences.

Heroes and heroines

The general impression gained from the book of Joshua of a wholesale violent conquest of the land of Canaan is somewhat mitigated by the story of the Shechem gathering and the admission of local groups to the covenant with Yahweh. These people are perhaps to be identified with the social group of the *habiru* mentioned in contemporary correspondence between local chiefs and their Egyptian overlords. These may have joined forces with Israel and merged into the new tribal union. A similar picture of Israel's infiltration into the land of Canaan can be derived from the book of Judges.

The stereotyped presentation of events in the book considers that the sin of the people is punished by the onslaught of an enemy tribe, which in turn is ended by the intervention of a judge called by God to deliver the people. This pattern of events, constantly repeated in the book, allows for the expression of the simplistic theology of the deuteronomistic editors, which has its roots in the book of Deuteronomy, that evil and disobedience to the law bring punishment, while goodness and obedience bring prosperity.

The first substantial tradition in the book, if we pass over the story of Ehud's assassination of the fat king of Moab in Judges chapter 3, is the story of Deborah. Deborah is described as judge and prophetess in Judges 4:4. She takes no part in the hostilities but attempts to inject some courage into the timorous Israelite army-commander Barak. Barak is quite obviously petrified of his forthcoming encounter with Sisera, the Canaanite commander of the army of king Jabin. Barak engages battle with Sisera in the vicinity of mount Tabor, but it is Yahweh who wins the victory for him. The portrayal of the strong woman Deborah is swiftly followed by that of another, Jael the Kenite. She it is who invites the fleeing Sisera to rest in her tent. She it is who kills him by driving a tent peg into his temple as he lies exhausted.

The story in Judges chapter 4 is followed by an ancient poem celebrating the same events. The poem praises Deborah, 'a mother in Israel', but gives the richest praise for Jael, stressing how Sisera fell at her hands by extraordinary repetition in 5:27. 'At her feet he bowed, he fell, he lay. At her feet he bowed, he fell. Where he bowed, there he fell slain.' But the poem is not without compassion. It has time to show sympathy for the mother of Sisera as she waits expectantly for her son to return victorious. This touch of unexpected pathos shows an awareness of human pain. The victory of one group inflicts grief on others. The killing of one person traumatises another. However laudable courage in the face of the enemy may be, it also multiplies grief and fuels antagonism.

The call of Gideon as a judge over Israel in Judges chapter 6 is long and detailed. His task is to confront the menace from the Midianites with his army of thirty-two thousand men. The story has Yahweh reduce this number to three hundred, so that it will be seen that the victory over Midian was the work of God not of Israel. Gideon is consequently asked to rule as king over the tribes of Israel. His answer in 8:23 is 'I will not rule over you, nor will my son. Yahweh will rule over you.' The issue of the appropriateness of kingship in Israel is raised. Should a nation ruled over by God have a king? Despite Gideon's refusal, his son Abimelech has all but one of his seventy brothers killed and himself proclaimed king. In a seemingly obscure text in chapter 9 the surviving brother Jotham likens Abimelech to a thorn bush. While some trees, the olive, the fig tree and the vine, refuse to lord it over the other trees, the worthless thorn bush seizes the crown. After three years of rule a revolt leads to the end of this sad experiment in monarchy. Monarchy is seen at this point as the unnecessary elevation of one man over others, a prize desired only by the unscrupulous.

Another of the major judges whose story is told in Judges chapters 11-12 is Jephthah, raised up to fight the Ammonites. It is Jephthah who makes a foolish and unnecessary bargain with God to offer in sacrifice the first living creature to meet him on his victorious return from fighting the enemy. The Ammonites are defeated, but it is Jephthah's daughter who meets him on his arrival home. 'His daughter came out to meet him with music and dancing. She was his only child. He had no son nor daughter but her.' (11:34) It is this unnamed daughter who is the true heroine of the story. She complies serenely with his stupid promise. After two months he does to her according to his vow. There is a nobility about the daughter of Jephthah which contrasts starkly with her father. The story speaks of the perceived sacredness of vows made to Yahweh, but also of a chronic disregard for the value of a human life, in this case the life of an innocent girl. Her willingness to become a holocaust to God recalls the attitude of Isaac bound as a sacrifice by Abraham. In this case, however, no angel intervenes to save the girl's life. The Genesis story illustrated the unacceptability of child sacrifice. The story of Jephthah's daughter betrays a primitive

morality with no apparent awareness that certain values, such as
the value of life, are to be defended above lesser values. The storyteller does not condemn Jephthah. The fate of Jephthah's daughter
recalls that of countless people, particularly women and children,
both in the past and in the present day, whose lives are brutally
ended due to primitive morality and prejudice.

The cycle of stories concerning Samson differs from those of
other judges, for Samson does not lead an army against the enemies
of Israel. Samson fights alone. He is called a judge, and the story of a
messenger of God announcing his birth states that he will be the
one who will begin to rescue Israel from the Philistines (13:5). These
new enemies of Israel, who probably originated in the Greek
islands, had begun to settle on the Mediterranean coastal plain at
this time. They represented a significant and continuing threat to
the emerging Israelite nation. The stories of Samson tell of his
escapades with various women, his acts of bravado such as tearing
a lion apart, his liking for riddles and his single-handed and pecu-
liar encounters with bands of Philistines.

When Delilah finally discovers the secret of his great strength
and betrays Samson to the Philistines, he is captured, blinded and
taken to Gaza. The stories have stressed that the spirit of Yahweh is
with him in his feats of strength (14:6, 14:19, 15:14) and Samson calls
on Yahweh for a last time when he is being taunted at a banquet in
Gaza. His strength renewed, he brings the building down on all the
guests and dies with them. 'The dead he killed at his death were
more than those he killed in his life.' (16:30) The stories of Samson
seem to come from popular story-telling. He tackles the Philistine
threat alone, makes several conquests among local women and dies
heroically. It may perhaps be debated to what extent Samson's
activities were driven by the spirit of Yahweh.

There was no king in Israel
The final chapters of the book of Judges do not introduce more
heroes and heroines. Instead two long tales are recorded of the time
before the kingship was established in Israel. 'In those days there
was no king in Israel; every man did what was right in his eyes.'

(17:6) These words are repeated three times in these chapters (18:1 19:1 21:25). The implication is that anarchy reigned, there being no judge and no king. The second of the two stories, which concerns the crime at Gibeah and its consequences, is a particularly gruesome tale of violence and killing.

A more benign and gentle story, which, though probably from later centuries, is set in the time of the judges, is to be found in the small book of Ruth. It tells of the emigration of a family from the tribe of Judah and the town of Bethlehem to the land of Moab. When the father of the family and the sons, who have married Moabite women, all in their turn have died, Naomi the mother is left as the only Israelite. Her daughter-in-law, Ruth, is determined to stay with her and support her. She speaks these memorable words: 'Where you go, I will go. Where you live, I will live. Your people is my people. Your God is my God. Where you die, I will die, and there I will be buried.' (Ruth 1:16-17) This vow of Ruth tells us the whole story. Ruth chooses to adhere to the God of Israel due to her faithful love for Naomi.

On their return to Bethlehem at the beginning of the barley harvest Ruth in her turn encounters kindness. A relation of Naomi, whose name is Boaz, in accordance with ancient practice, allows Ruth to glean from his own fields. Ruth is now both a widow and a foreigner and so has double claim to be treated with compassion in Israel. Ruth sleeps at Boaz's feet that night to symbolise her wish for him to 'redeem' her from her situation as a widow of his clan by marrying her. Boaz obtains the refusal of a kinsman who has a prior claim to her and takes Ruth as his wife.

The story of Ruth reflects the inferior position of women in this early time, but the goodness of Ruth and her fidelity call forth the kindness of Boaz. Such people are the true heroes and heroines of any society. Boaz and Ruth achieve historical importance as the parents of Obed, father of Jesse, father of David, but it is their fidelity and kindness which is celebrated in the book. The book of Ruth demonstrates an appreciation of foreigners which may perhaps indicate a later origin than the time of the judges, but it provides a welcome counterbalance to the battles and violence reported elsewhere. The quiet presence of God in the everyday lives of ordinary people speaks more powerfully than the supposed assistance of God fighting with Joshua and Samson.

CHAPTER 5

Saul and David

During the time of the judges, which we can estimate as being from 1200 to 1000 BC, the people of Israel gradually established themselves in more and more areas of the land of Canaan. They had enemies to contend with, who were considered to have been sent by Yahweh to bring punishment on Israel. They had charismatic leaders who inspired resistance to their oppressors. They remained in a loose federation of tribes who joined forces when necessary. They had also considered the possibility of forging a more united union by choosing themselves a king.

The Philistines seem to have posed the most significant threat to Israel as this period drew to its end. A loose federation of tribes still faced a formidable enemy from the Mediterranean coastal plain. In the first of the two books of Samuel, which continues the story from the book of Judges, the Philistine presence remains menacing.

Samuel, prophet and judge
It is somewhat misleading that the next two books of the deuteronomistic history are both called books of Samuel. Samuel is present in much of the first book, but dies before the book ends. The second book of Samuel is taken up principally with the reign of David.

The story of Samuel begins with the plight of Hannah, one of the two wives of Elkanah, who had remained childless. On visiting Shiloh, where the ark of the covenant is kept, Hannah prays for a son. Her prayer is answered and Samuel is born. Once he is weaned Hannah takes Samuel to Shiloh and entrusts him to the priest Eli. Samuel would sleep in the sanctuary at Shiloh and a story of his being called by God in this place is recorded. Three times God calls. Three times Samuel runs to Eli, thinking it was he who had sum-

moned him. Eli finally tells Samuel to reply to the voice, 'Speak,
Yahweh, your servant is listening' (1 Samuel 3:9).

This willingness to receive words from God is the beginning of
Samuel's career as a prophet, one who hears from God and speaks
for God. 'Yahweh was with him, and he let no word of his fall to the
ground' (1 Samuel 3:19). It is true that Moses had been considered a
friend of God and prophet, for God spoke to him face to face
(Numbers 12:6-8, Deuteronomy 34:10), but Samuel is the first of a
long line of prophets, some close to the rulers of Israel, others
deeply opposed to them, but all regarded as speaking for God in
changing circumstances.

The Philistine threat has not gone away. After defeat by the
Philistines the Israelites decide to bring the ark of the covenant from
Shiloh to join the army. The ark of God is captured at this encounter
in which thirty thousand Israelites are said to have perished. The
traditions of Yahweh fighting holy war with Israel take on a new
form here. By taking the ark of God into battle the Israelites believe
they can force a victory. This tradition seems to point out that God
cannot be constrained to fight for the people, nor is God contained
in an ark. The ark is only the sign of the presence of God among the
Israelites. Solomon will show similar understanding when on inau-
gurating the temple in Jerusalem he prays to the God who cannot
be contained.

As 1 Samuel chapter 5 then narrates, the capture of the ark and
its removal to the temple of the god Dagan in the town of Ashdod
leads to God's punishment of the Philistines. On two successive
mornings the statue of Dagan lies comically prostrate before the
ark, and on the second morning the head and hands have been sev-
ered. A plague breaks out among the Philistines which produces
painful tumours. Just as the Israelites cannot manipulate God with
impunity, similarly the Philistines do not go unpunished when they
attempt to reduce Yahweh to an impotent local deity. Having trans-
ferred the ark from town to town, the Philistines have it returned to
the Israelites, though not to the sanctuary of Shiloh which they have
destroyed.

The hostilities between Israel and the Philistines have revealed

Israel's weakness and demands for a king begin to be voiced in earnest. 'Give us a king to rule us like all the nations,' they say to Samuel (8:5). In the material from 1 Samuel chapter 8 to chapter 12 the issue of choosing a king dominates the story, and the biblical text betrays the struggle to decide whether kingship is acceptable in Israel or not. Gideon the judge had refused kingship in deference to Yahweh the king. Samuel the judge and prophet has similar misgivings, which are presented also in words of Yahweh to him: 'they have not rejected you but me from ruling over them' (8:7).

Theological difficulties with the idea of a king are compounded by fears of the social consequences of kingship. Samuel addresses the people on the disadvantages of the kingship in words which seem to reflect the later experience of Israel. Kings levy taxes. Kings conscript men for military service and forced labour. Kings enslave women in their courts and in their harems. Such material which emphasises the evil effects of monarchy is accompanied by the narrative of the anointing of Saul by Samuel. It is Yahweh who instructs Samuel to anoint this man from the tribe of Benjamin with the explicit mission of saving the people from the power of the Philistines (9:16). This seems rather reminiscent of the raising of judges to deal with a particular military threat. And yet, in a subsequent passage, Samuel again declares that anointing a king is tantamount to rejecting God (10:19). Finally, when Saul wins a victory over the Ammonites, all the people acclaim him as their king (11:15).

The issue of the appropriateness of kingship for a nation ruled by God is relevant in all historical periods. To what extent does acclamation of a human leader entail abdication of free conscientious choice in response to God's law? Israel had problems with kingship and Saul paid dearly for the lack of wholehearted support. But Israel would eventually consider the king to be God's chosen one and thus reconcile the tension of the two kingships of Yahweh and the king. Was this really God's will, or a compromise?

The rise and fall of Saul
It is noteworthy that the narratives of the choosing of a king do not

usually use the Hebrew word for 'king', *melek*. Even in the accounts which support the establishment of the monarchy there is a prefer- ence for the less exalted role of *nagid*, which means 'leader'. God's instruction to Samuel reads, 'You will anoint him as leader over my people Israel' (9:16). This reluctance to describe Saul as *melek* seems to reflect the theological and social misgivings about the monarchy. The anti-monarchy texts, in describing the negative consequences of kingship (8:10-18) and in having the crowd shout 'Long live the king' (10:24), simply add to the sense of unease regarding the term. The prophet Hosea will in later times echo such misgivings in alluding to the making of a king as a serious crime (Hosea 9:15).

Despite this lack of wholehearted support Saul achieves victo- ries as leader of Israel, rather as the judges did. The first book of Samuel gives detailed accounts of his victories against the Philistines and against the Amalekites, a nomadic people already encountered by Moses on the journey to Sinai. Amid these stories we discover two separate accounts of Samuel's rejection of Saul. When preparing to fight the Philistines Saul waits for seven days for the arrival of Samuel who is due to offer sacrifices before the battle. When Samuel does not arrive Saul offers the sacrifices him- self. Samuel's reaction on his arrival informs Saul that God has already chosen another leader (13:14). When the people keep back the best of the animals of the Amalekites from the ban of destruc- tion and spare Agag their king, there is a second occasion for Samuel to condemn Saul (15:22-23). Saul's reign is thus crippled from the start. By well-meaning but perhaps foolish deeds he loses the support of Samuel, if he ever had it. Furthermore, this first incumbent of the new monarchy was never favoured by circum- stances. The narratives explain, with reference to God's choice and God's rejection, the sad and all too human story of Saul's reign.

The plight of unfortunate Saul is in no way helped when David comes on the scene. A man who is clearly inadequate for his job and who has lacked the necessary support of those with authority and influence is now further undermined by the arrival of the ideal can- didate for the throne. Samuel is sent by Yahweh to Bethlehem to anoint a son of Jesse. God's choice is of the youngest, described as having 'fine eyes and good looks' (16:12). As the story unfolds we are aware that David is the writer's hero. Though he feels some sympathy for Saul, David is a winner. The portrayal of Saul and David is a reflection of human adulation of heroes and heroines, and neglect and rejection of those who fail. Saul can do nothing right from now on.

Once David has been anointed and has received the spirit of Yahweh Saul is prey to an 'evil spirit' from Yahweh (16:14). To soothe Saul's depression a young harpist, the very same David, is employed by Saul. He wins Saul's favour. A separate tradition introduces David afresh as bringing supplies to his brothers who have joined Saul's army. As David arrives in the camp the Philistine fighter Goliath is issuing his challenge to single combat to resolve the hostilities between Israelites and Philistines. The triumph of David narrated in 1 Samuel chapter 17 further undermines Saul, who begins to menace David. He encourages David to further deeds of valour in the hope that he will one day be killed.

David's friendship with Jonathan, Saul's son, shows Jonathan as not sharing his father's jealousy and resentment of David's talents. Jonathan acts as mediator between the two rivals, and eventually arranges David's escape. That David is now free to plot against him unhinges Saul's mind. His massacre of the priests of Nob who helped David and his desperate attempt to have the dead Samuel conjured up by the witch of Endor are the final stages on the road to his tragic death after facing the Philistines on mount Gilboa. With Saul die Jonathan and two other sons of Saul.

The tale of the tragedy of Saul is told with a certain sympathy for this first disastrous king. But we may be uneasy with the picture of Saul chosen by Yahweh yet rejected without being given a proper chance, and driven then by an evil spirit from Yahweh. Are not the writers of the Saul tradition too sure about God's role in the rise and fall of Saul?

The reign of David

The reports of the death of Saul conflict in the details of how he died, whether by his own hand or by the hand of an Amalekite Saul asked to kill him. What is in no doubt, as the second book of Samuel begins, is that David reacts in a way designed to profit considerably by the death. David's affection for Jonathan and Saul seems genuine if one reads the lament given in 2 Samuel chapter 1. From this poem comes the proverb 'How are the mighty fallen'. David laments both the courage and the human qualities of Saul and Jonathan. But David's execution of the Amalekite who claimed to have killed Saul is a move designed to win the support of Saul's followers.

David's rise to power is now rapid. The men of Judah are quick to anoint David king over their tribe. There is no hesitation in using the title *melek*. After internal wranglings among the remnant of Saul's house the men of the other tribes of Israel ask David to be their king too. David thus unites the two entities of Judah and the other tribes of Israel in his own person. Reluctance about having a king is now forgotten. The traditions about David can present him in no other way.

The first shrewd move of the new king of Judah and Israel is to capture the Jebusite city of Jerusalem. The city had already been mentioned in Egyptian texts and it now begins its long and traumatic history as a city of the Israelites. The city lay in neither Judah nor Israel, and its choice therefore did nothing to fuel jealousies. David arranges furthermore for the ark to be brought to Jerusalem so that it becomes the religious as well as the political centre of the united kingdom.

Perhaps the most important chapter in the story of David's reign is the seventh chapter of 2 Samuel. For the first time we encounter the prophet Nathan, a court prophet who is resolute in passing on to David words welcome and unwelcome. The chapter raises the issue of building a temple for Yahweh in Jerusalem. Having at first agreed to the plan, Nathan is warned in a dream to forbid the king to build a temple. Rather like the issue of kingship, which the Israelites came to accept, the question of building a temple as other nations had for their gods also raised serious theological problems. Should the religion of Yahweh imitate the ways of pagan nations? Was it appropriate to appear to contain God in a man-made sanctu-

ary? Just as the idea of monarchy was at first rejected, so the project
of building a temple for God is shelved.

There is more to Nathan's speech than this. In an elaborate
word-play Nathan declares that David is not to build a house for
God but that God will build a house for David (7:11). The Hebrew
word *bet* is used both for the house of God and for the royal house
of David. This promise is valid for David and his descendants. Even
if they do evil, the solidarity of God will not pass from David's
royal house. Israel has come to terms with kingship. The king is no
rival to Yahweh. He is rather Yahweh's anointed one. He is a son of
God (7:14). This is the beginning of the phenomenon of the messiah
and the idealised presentations that will accompany it. Israel casts
aside all its misgivings about kingship and embraces the monarchy
as a God-given institution. Even inadequate and evil kings of
Judah, of whom Manasseh is the classic example, will be considered
anointed ones of God. But the experience of inadequate kings will
fuel the messianic idealism which finds expression in the psalms
belonging to royal liturgies and in the hopes for the future
expressed by many prophets. Hopes for an ideal king, as David was
considered to have been, are encouraged. The idea of a covenant
with David will naturally emerge from such developments (Psalm
89:3). God promises solidarity with David's line as he once
promised his gifts to Abraham, Isaac and Jacob.

The reports about the reign of David in the second book of
Samuel show how David established a court and a civil service. He
had his own personal troops and officials in charge of forced
labour, initially only for foreigners. The story of David taking a cen-
sus is reported in very negative terms. That David should count the
people for the purposes of taxation and conscription can be understood as reprehensible, but the punishment brought on the people
is not explained.

Much of the story in the second book of Samuel concerns directly
or indirectly the problem of the succession. Some scholars go so far
as to call the material from 2 Samuel chapter 9 to 1 Kings chapter 2
the 'succession narrative'. It is perhaps better seen as an account of
the family and court life of David. The compilers took considerable

risks in reporting the sordid details of the life of this royal family, the most notorious episode of which is David's affair with Bathsheba.

The story of David and Bathsheba opens with the words 'at the turn of the year, when kings go to war' (11:1). While David's army commander Joab lays siege to Rabbah of the Ammonites, David remains in Jerusalem. The story of David's sighting of Bathsheba and summoning this wife of Uriah the Hittite to his palace is among the most well-known of biblical stories. The honesty of the editors of these books allows us to see a man apparently chosen by God for a special purpose and yet prey to serious human weaknesses. David's sin of adultery is compounded by his treatment of Uriah. The psychological insight of the writer is notable when David endeavours repeatedly to make Uriah go down to his house to sleep with his wife. That Uriah should go down to his house becomes an obsession for David, and the phrase is repeated in statements and questions: has he gone down? he has not gone down (11:8-11). David then resorts to arranging the killing of Uriah when he returns to the battle for Rabbah.

The continuation of the story brings the masterly confrontation of David by Nathan his prophet. The same man who promised a dynasty to David now cleverly traps David into admitting his guilt. The story of the poor man's ewe lamb has David condemn himself. Nathan rounds on David with the words 'You are the man!' (12:7). The story, in addition to admitting the human weakness of David, also attempts to explain David's subsequent family difficulties. The problems created for David by members of his family are considered to be punishment for his sin. While a connection between David's behaviour as father of the family and the behaviour of his sons is not to be denied, one is also aware here of an attempt to explain the misfortunes of the family history of God's anointed king by reference to David's sins.

A lesser known incident in David's family history is recounted in 2 Samuel 13. David's first-born son Amnon is consumed with passion for his half-sister Tamar. Feigning illness he asks that Tamar be brought to care for him. He overpowers and rapes his sister. Once again the narrator shows deep psychological insight in telling the sordid tale. In due time Absalom, Tamar's brother, kills Amnon and flees to the king of Geshur, his mother's father, in the land to the east of the Sea of Galilee. Absalom is finally reconciled to David but plans a rebellion. He uses the divisions between Judah and the northern tribes of Israel to gain support from disgruntled people in the north. Once Absalom has himself proclaimed king, David leaves Jerusalem without a fight. The ultimate punishment of David's sins comes when Absalom usurps David's harem (16:22). The judgement of Nathan, as recorded in the family history, now includes reference to this deed (12:11-12). It is a punishment which fits the crime of David.

Absalom's revolt ends in the disaster of Absalom's death and the king's grief-stricken return to Jerusalem. Further differences between the people of the two kingdoms lead to the revolt of Sheba, a man of the tribe of Benjamin, and the last days of David are marked by the attempt of Adonijah, fourth son of David, to seize the throne. A jealous Bathsheba, whose second son by David, Solomon, has been brought up at the court, ensures with the help of Nathan that it is Solomon who takes the throne.

The history of the early years of the dynasty of David presents events to challenge faith in the God who chose such a man and such a family. But the honesty of the tradition is even more striking. It seems to be affirming that God chooses weak human beings despite their weakness. The strength of the belief in God's choice of David is even clearer when we read the parallel history of David in the chronicler's history. In these historical books, written possibly only after the return from exile in Babylon, the writers use material from 1 and 2 Samuel when considering David, but anything negative on David is omitted, for the chroniclers see him as the saintly founder of the Jerusalem temple, a priestly king.

In the version in Chronicles the story of the siege of Rabbah of the Ammonites is exceedingly brief, for the whole episode of Bathsheba and Uriah has been left out (1 Chronicles 20:1-3). There is no report of the rape of Tamar, the murder of Amnon, the revolt and death of Absalom and the revolt of Sheba the Benjaminite. David's advice to Solomon to eliminate all his enemies, reported in

1 Kings 2, has no place in the Chronicles. The first book of Chronicles provides instead chapter on chapter concerning David's preparation for the building of the temple and its services. Even though the temple was not built until Solomon's time, the credit goes to David. David's love for God is also accentuated by the attribution to him of many psalms. The memory that he was a harpist combines with his desire to build a temple to make him an irresistible candidate as composer of sacred music.

David is a complex and attractive figure. While the deuteronomistic history in the second book of Samuel honestly reflects his talents and his troubles, the later tradition canonises and idolises David. The realistic portrayal of David illustrates how God may choose weak individuals to achieve great things. The idealised presentations of later traditions may speak more of human beings' need for perfect models. It is fortunate that the honest accounts of David's life have not been silenced by later trends.

CHAPTER 6

Solomon and other kings

The talent of David sees the monarchy firmly established. Religious misgivings about monarchy have been put aside. It has become acceptable to regard the king as God's anointed one. The question of building a temple has still to be resolved, but the united kingdom of Judah and Israel is gradually shaping itself into a state like the other nations. As in the other nations too, royalty is revered and idolised, but royalty cannot live up to the high ideals expected of it. The family of king David has more than its share of immorality and violence. The history of David's reign is not a happy story. From all this there emerges a son of David who has won the throne due to the intrigue of his mother and the collaboration of David's prophet. After the uncertainties of David's later years 'the kingdom of Solomon was securely established' (1 Kings 2:12).

Solomon the magnificent
David's death has scarcely been reported when the story turns to Solomon's elimination of all opposition. His half-brother Adonijah, who had attempted to seize the throne before David's death, is murdered when he requests David's concubine Abishag for himself. David's commander Joab consequently fears for his life. Despite Joab's taking refuge in the tent where the ark of the covenant is lodged Joab is still ruthlessly murdered at Solomon's command. Solomon even eliminates the harmless Shimei, who had insulted David during the revolt of Absalom. Once these security measures have been carried out the text reaffirms: 'and the kingdom was established in the hand of Solomon' (1 Kings 2:46).

In order to consolidate relations with foreign powers Solomon takes wives from various nations. He ensures cordial relations with

a weakened Egypt by marrying the daughter of the reigning
pharaoh. He even receives as a dowry from the pharaoh the city of
Gezer (9:16). His marriages to various pagan wives lead Solomon to
establish shrines for their gods alongside the temple of Yahweh. It
is this activity which the writers of 1 Kings see as justifying future
punishment for David's line in the division of the kingdom of Judah
and Israel. As happened with David's reign, negative developments
must be explained by some fault in the king. Solomon's women,
numbered as seven hundred royal wives and three hundred concu-
bines, sway his heart, and the king is said to become involved in the
worship of other gods (11:3). Needless to say, such details are omitted in 2 Chronicles.

Solomon fortifies towns throughout Israel. In the north east,
Hazor is partly rebuilt. Strategically situated Megiddo, which controls the valley of Jezreel and access towards the east from the
Mediterranean, is massively fortified. Such towns serve to protect
trade routes. And trade flourished in Solomon's day, both by land
and by sea. An alliance with king Hiram of Tyre allowed Solomon's
men to learn from Hiram's experienced sailors (9:27). The port of
Ezion-geber, near modern Eilat on the gulf of Aqaba, allowed for
trading relations with Arabia and Africa. As 1 Kings chapter 10 narrates, precious woods and precious stones, as well as ivory and
baboons are among the items traded. Copper was produced and
traded, and Solomon's traders became middlemen in the commerce
of horses and chariots. The Queen of Sheba not only marvels at
Solomon's wisdom and achievements but also leads a trade delega-
tion.

The achievement of Solomon which is given the most attention
is the building of the temple. Four chapters describe the construction and decoration of the temple and its solemn opening, though it
is noted that while the temple took seven years to build, Solomon's
palace took thirteen (6:38, 7:1). As it became reconciled to kingship,
so Israel accepted the construction of a temple after the style of
pagan buildings. It is underlined, however, in the prayer of
Solomon at the temple's dedication, that this building constructed
by human hands can never contain the God of heaven and earth

(8:27). Solomon continues his prayer and speaks of those who would seek God in the temple in times of war, famine, or plague. But the temple is also to be the house of prayer of the foreigner, where his prayer too can be answered (8:42). The prayer of Solomon encompasses later reflection about the temple. It is not only the place of sacrifice, but a place of prayer in time of individual and community need, and even a place of prayer for all nations. The words of the prophet in Isaiah 56:7 are anticipated here.

The dedication of the temple is accompanied by innumerable sacrifices. One text speaks in exaggerated fashion of twenty-two thousand sheep (8:63). The response of God is a renewal of the promises made to David, but with a major difference. God's promise is no longer unconditional. The statement 'I will never take back my love', found in Nathan's oracle to David, does not appear. If the commandments are not obeyed Yahweh threatens to cut Israel off from the land and cast out the temple from God's presence (9:7). It seems that these words of Yahweh to Solomon presuppose the events of the exile, the loss of the land and the destruction of the temple. The promise of God to David was unconditional. The promise to David's son suggests God might take action against the people. The trauma of the exile to Babylon had a profound effect on Israel's theology, and leads to this new form of God's promise to the king.

The time of Solomon, with the monarchy firmly established, provides opportunities for a flowering of culture. There is evidence of writing from this time. Solomon has secretaries to record royal decisions and events. There is reference to the 'book of the acts of Solomon', which unfortunately has never been retrieved (11:41). With the establishment of court life and court officials it may well be true that other traditions were put into writing and edited in Solomon's reign. The history of David's rise to power and the story of his reign, now preserved in the books of Samuel, may well have been written down at this time. Many scholars believe that the material in the Pentateuch commonly described as 'yahwist' was put into written form in Solomon's day. This material reflects the new national confidence and the influence of neighbouring nations.

Solomon is renowned for his wisdom and is remembered as a collector of proverbs. It is quite plausible that the first collections of wise sayings which found their way into the book of Proverbs were compiled at this time. Furthermore, with the building of the temple, collections of psalms were probably made. The first stages of many biblical books may well date to the time of Solomon.

The seeds of division

This so-called 'golden age' was not without its problems. Solomon's style of living required taxation. In the northern kingdom of Israel Solomon set up twelve administrative districts. Each district would provide produce for the royal court for one month of each year (4:7). Building activity led to forced labour. David had used foreigners for this and Solomon continues to enslave vassal peoples from neighbouring nations. But he also arranges the conscription of Israelites (5:27/5:13). The people of Judah, it seems, were exempt from both taxation and conscription (11:28).

Serious divisions begin to appear between north and south, and between the levels of society. Those associated with the king and the court can profit from Solomon's favour. They can imitate Solomon's unjust treatment of his subjects. The seeds of division are well and truly sown. At this point it begins to be seen that Judah and Israel are losing the vision of a society of equals provided for by the laws of the covenant. A society in which the covenant of Yahweh provides for all in equal measure is replaced by a nation in which the king has absolute power.

For all Solomon's reputation for wisdom, he also demonstrates considerable foolishness in his unequal treatment of the people of Israel and the people of Judah. As it did with David, the tradition emphasises Solomon's good qualities. But the first book of Kings does not hide the fact that his policies spelt disaster and division for the kingdoms recently united under his father David. Tribal independence has been lost and the new system of administration has furthered division. The tradition blames Solomon principally for religious faults. His wives seduce him into pagan practices (11:4). Such developments undoubtedly undermined the cohesion of the nation, but it seems that oppressive social measures were the major contributing factor to the ensuing breaking up of the united kingdom.

The story of the splitting up of the united kingdom is told in 1 Kings chapter 12. But this event is prepared for in the story of Ahijah the prophet in the previous chapter. Ahijah was from Shiloh, the cultic centre where the ark had been lodged and where the prophet Samuel had been called. Ahijah therefore represents the old order, swept away by Solomon and his temple. Ahijah it is who designates Jeroboam, who had been in charge of forced labour for the northern tribes, to seize the northern kingdom from Solomon's successor. Ahijah the prophet is involved in the political situation of the northern kingdom, just as Nathan, David's prophet, had played a major role in the events of David's rule. Ahijah gives his instructions to Jeroboam divine authority. It is Yahweh who will tear one kingdom from the hands of Solomon's son (11:31).

The prophetic phenomenon in Israel reaches its climax in the individual prophets to whom books of the Old Testament have been attributed. But it has its roots in earlier times and in practices shared by neighbouring nations. Early prophets, such as the bands of prophets found in the story of Saul, were described as being possessed by the spirit of Yahweh. They were liable to behave in frenzied and uncontrolled ways. They were also accustomed to performing symbolic actions to communicate God's word. Ahijah of Shiloh is wearing a new cloak when he goes to meet Jeroboam (11:29). Ahijah tears the cloak into twelve strips, ten of which he gives to Jeroboam. The ten strips represent the northern tribes, while the two represent the tribe of Judah and possibly the tribe of Simeon which had been absorbed by Judah. This action communicates the message in a more forceful way. Ahijah then explains the action as symbolising God's judgement on Solomon's idolatry. Solomon is to keep Judah for the sake of David. The story of Ahijah allows us to see the prophet's involvement in political manoevrings, but also gives the theological explanation of the division of the kingdom. The story of the assembly at Shechem which follows in 1 Kings 12 provides the social reasons for the split.

On the death of Solomon, Rehoboam his son becomes king of
Judah. He travels to Shechem in the centre of the northern kingdom
to be declared king of Israel. At this point the grievances of the
northerners can be voiced. Appeals are made to Rehoboam to lighten
the burden of national service. But Rehoboam is young and inexper-
ienced and heeds the advice of his peers, who advise him to say:
'My little finger is thicker than my father's loins' (12:10). Rehoboam
promises to make heavier the heavy burden Solomon had laid on
the people. Such is the foolish reply of Rehoboam to the people of
the north. Secession follows. 'What share have we in David?' is
their reply (12:16). When Rehoboam sends Adoniram, a new official,
to organise conscription, the people of Israel stone him to death.
The foolishness of Solomon is compounded by the foolishness of
his son.

The editors of the material manage to explain the historical division of the two kingdoms by referring to God's judgement. They
are able to maintain the fidelity of God to David's line by leaving
the tribe of Judah to Solomon's son. Their regard for the promise to
David leads them to portray the northern kingdom as seditious and
unfaithful from the start. The chronicler's history goes even further
and does not even mention the two centuries of autonomous existence of the northern kingdom.

The divided kingdom

Solomon's son, Rehoboam, is warned by yet another prophet,
Shemaiah, to accept the division of the kingdom as God's doing
(12:22-24). Jeroboam is acclaimed as first king of the north. From
this point and for the next two hundred years it is customary to
refer to the northern kingdom as 'Israel'. The pretext needed by the
historical writers of 1 Kings to turn against Jeroboam is provided by
his religious policy. The independent nation of Israel cannot allow
its citizens to travel to the temple in Jerusalem for worship.
Jeroboam designates two ancient sites, Bethel and Dan, as cultic
centres, one in the south of the kingdom and one in the north.
According to 1 Kings 12:28-30, golden calves are set up at each
shrine. The writer seems deliberately to misrepresent Jeroboam at

this point. He draws parallels with the account of the apostasy in the desert, when Aaron fashioned the golden calf and had the people worship it (Exodus 32). Such provision of images by Jeroboam might simply be compared to the *kerubim* designed by Solomon for the Holy of Holies in the Jerusalem temple. It may have been unwise that Jeroboam had adopted the bull symbol of local religions, but the prejudice of the writers against northern religion is obvious from the start.

For the historians who wrote up these traditions from their own perspective as Judahites, Jeroboam and the subsequent kings of Israel can do no good. They report on the reigns of kings of Israel with a stereotyped dismissal: 'He did what was evil in the sight of Yahweh. He walked in the way of Jeroboam who made Israel sin' (15:26, 15:34, etc.). There are sporadic clashes between Israel and Judah. Israel is far less stable, with frequent coups and assassinations. The kingdom of Judah, though it enjoys some stability with the davidic kings, suffers invasion from a resurgent Egypt soon after the death of Solomon. The pharaoh Shishak even robs the temple in Jerusalem of its treasures (14:25-26). Some stability is eventually regained by the northern kingdom under the rule of Omri and his successors. It is in this period, during the reign of Ahab son of Omri, that the great prophet Elijah comes on the scene.

Ahab and Elijah

Elijah is arguably the most celebrated of the prophets of Israel. Though he is not one of those to whom a book is attributed and few words of Elijah are recorded, his deeds in confronting Ahab king of Israel and his wife Jezebel mark him as the mightiest of prophets. Elijah the Tishbite, from Tishbe in Gilead, appears out of the blue to confront Ahab. The stories of Elijah, which seem to have existed as a separate collection of tales before being inserted in the history of the kings, begin in 1 Kings chapter 17. Shortly before this the historian had delivered the stereotyped judgement for kings of Israel in regard to Ahab. He too did what was displeasing to Yahweh. He too followed the example of Jeroboam, who led Israel into sin. But in addition to all this Ahab had married Jezebel, the daughter of the king of Sidon (16:31). Ahab gave free rein to Jezebel, who set out to establish the worship of Baal and destroy the worship of Yahweh. The Hebrew word *ba'al* means 'lord' or 'master' and is used of the local gods of Tyre and Sidon and also of the local Canaanite gods. It seems that such pagan worship was never fully eradicated from Israel. The prophet Hosea will devote a lot of energy to opposing the worship of the Canaanite gods.

With Jezebel behind him Ahab builds a temple to the Baal of Tyre in Samaria, the new capital of the northern kingdom established by Omri, his father. What is apparently a struggle between Elijah and Ahab is in fact a confrontation between worship of Yahweh and worship of pagan gods. Jezebel is the power behind Ahab's throne. With shorter and longer tales the struggle between the prophet and his enemies is told.

Elijah begins by declaring a drought from Yahweh (17:1). It is Yahweh and not Baal who provides the rain. It is Yahweh and not Baal who withholds it. During the three-year drought Elijah further demonstrates the supremacy of Yahweh by working wonders. Elijah himself is fed by ravens. He then miraculously provides food for a widow at Zarephath, a town of Sidon. He thus demonstrates that Yahweh has power even in the land of the Sidonian Baal. When the same widow's son dies, Elijah raises him to life. Yahweh, not the local baal, has sway over life and death in Sidon as elsewhere.

At the end of the three-year drought the most dramatic confrontation takes place. The four hundred and fifty prophets of Baal are summoned to Mount Carmel to meet Elijah, the only remaining prophet of Yahweh. The other prophets of Yahweh have apparently been slaughtered by Jezebel (18:4). Elijah challenges the prophets of Baal to call down fire on a bull prepared for sacrifice. 'The god who answers with fire is god indeed,' declares Elijah (18:24). The story of Elijah and the prophets of Baal presents a sarcastic Elijah ridiculing his rivals. As the four hundred and fifty prophets enter into a frenzy of prayer, dancing and self-mutilation, Elijah encourages them to call louder to wake up their god. But there is no voice, no answer (18:29). Elijah has the bull he prepares for sacrifice doused in water. At his prayer fire consumes the bull, the wood and the water. The people's reaction is to cry 'Yahweh is God', echoing Elijah's very name, which means 'my God is Yahweh'. Elijah slaughters the prophets of Baal in accordance with holy war rules. The stories in these first two chapters of the Elijah cycle illustrate the prophet's fundamental claim that Yahweh is the true god. Elijah is as ferocious as Jezebel.

A more uplifting story of Elijah is the tale of his journey to the mountain of God. In 1 Kings chapter 19 Elijah travels for forty days and forty nights to the mountain which northern tradition calls Horeb, the mountain known otherwise as Sinai. Moses had found God on this mountain, and Elijah has his strength renewed here. He travels there with food provided by an angel-messenger. The mighty Elijah discovers God on Horeb not in the wind, not in the earthquake, not in the fire, but in a still, small voice (19:11-12). No voice, no answer had been given to the raving prophets of Baal, but the true prophet of Yahweh listens for a still, small voice. The God who was understood as thundering on the mountain in the Sinai tradition of the Pentateuch is perceptible in the calm of a small voice in the tale of Elijah. The God who had whispered to the boy Samuel at Shiloh speaks in silence to Elijah on Horeb. The God of mighty clamour is also a God of quiet stillness. Elijah is sent from Sinai to continue his mission.

A dimension of prophecy which will develop in the writing prophets is social concern. The story of Naboth's vineyard in 1 Kings chapter 21 shows Elijah taking a stand against royal usurpation of land legitimately held by individual Israelites. It is Jezebel who encourages her husband to break the covenant laws and to disregard the rightful inheritance of Naboth. Ahab is portrayed as a weakling who mopes when Naboth refuses to sell his land to the king (21:4). But Jezebel has a plan and arranges for Naboth to be falsely accused of speaking against God and against the king, and to be stoned to death. Ahab recovers from his moping and takes possession of Naboth's vineyard. The sentence of Elijah is not long in coming. Where the dogs licked Naboth's blood they will lick Ahab's blood too (21:19). And a similar fate is prescribed for Jezebel. Elijah's intervention to defend the property rights of the individual is a new stage in prophetic social involvement. As prophets had criticised the behaviour of David and Solomon, so Elijah opposes Ahab. The tradition of defence of those whose rights are disregarded by the rich and powerful will continue with the writing prophets, in particular with Amos, Isaiah and Micah.

Elijah once more challenges belief in a local baal in the story of the illness of Ahab's son Ahaziah, narrated in 2 Kings chapter 1. The young king sends messengers to the shrine of the local god of Ekron. The god is described mockingly in the Hebrew text as *ba'al-zebub*, 'lord of the flies', which ridicules his title of *ba'al-zebul*, 'exalted lord'. Elijah intercepts the messengers and sends them back to Ahaziah. When the king three times sends a captain and fifty soldiers to summon Elijah, two of these contingents are devoured by fire from heaven. The third captain successfully pleads for the lives of his men. Elijah finally confronts the king to tell him that for consulting the god of Ekron he will die of his illness. In such features as the fire from heaven this story shows signs of popular storytelling, as did the tale of the prophets of Baal. Elijah is once again the prophet who declares by word and deed: 'my God is Yahweh'.

Elisha

Elisha had become the servant of Elijah on Elijah's return from Horeb. In 2 Kings chapter 2 Elijah takes his leave of his disciple. Elisha is unwilling to let his master depart alone. He requests a double share of Elijah's spirit. Elisha sees Elijah taken up to heaven in a chariot of fire, and is granted the double share. No trace of Elijah is found by the men who organise a search for him despite Elisha's opposition (2:17). Just as there had been no trace of Moses' grave, so there is no sign of Elijah. This disappearance to heaven of the mighty prophet seems to have given rise to the belief that he would return before the last days, a belief stated in the closing verses of the prophet Malachi.

Elisha's ministry is far less impressive than that of his master. Elaborate tales are told of the miracles he worked, some having close parallels to those of Elijah. He too demonstrates the concern of the God of Israel beyond the borders of Israel in the healing of

Naaman, the Syrian army commander in 2 Kings chapter 5. Naaman's concern to transport some soil of Israel on two mules back with him to Damascus shows the belief that each god has its own limited territory. Such ideas are beginning to be challenged in Israelite tradition.

While Elijah had been taken up to heaven, Elisha is buried. A final wonder is worked when a dead man returns to life after being deposited hurriedly in the tomb of Elisha (13:20-21). Despite such wonders it must be admitted that Elisha is something of a poor imitation of his mentor. Elijah stood for the God of heaven and earth, who nevertheless speaks to the human heart and whose laws defend the rights of each individual. Elisha, with his double share of the spirit, generally indulges in wonder-working for the genuine good of individuals. The story of the cursing of the small boys, however, suggests the scare tactics of a folktale (2:23-24). The invocation of Yahweh to curse the boys and the subsequent savagery does not enhance the relatively poor impact of Elisha. For both Elijah and Elisha we are provided with popular stories and legends. For later prophets the focus will be almost entirely on the prophetic word.

CHAPTER 7

Amos and Hosea

In the middle of the eighth century BC the phenomenon of prophecy undergoes an important change. Before this point the activities of prophets such as Nathan, Ahijah and the great Elijah are reported in the historical books of the Old Testament. From the eighth century onwards the scriptures provide separate books of the prophets. From what has been said of earlier prophets it will already be clear that the fundamental task of the prophet is to receive and pass on the word of God. There has been much reflection over centuries about how this process might work. It should suffice here to say that a prophet is one who is able to hear the word, and has the courage to proclaim what he hears. The prophet's lot is not a happy one, for the message will frequently fall on deaf ears.

The books of the Old Testament attributed to prophets were the final stages in a long process of development. We have very little information about this process. There are occasional references in the books of the prophets to the writing down of their speeches. The prophet Jeremiah has a scribe named Baruch to record his speeches, but we should beware of considering this as normal. It seems most plausible that the words of the prophets made a deep impression on people and that their words were written down by disciples who had remembered and preserved their teaching. The situation is similar to that of the development of traditions concerning Jesus of Nazareth. The initial impact leads to the memorising and preaching by disciples and subsequently to writing the teaching down for future generations. The texts of the prophets often suggest a development of teaching and additions from later editors. The final verses of the book of Amos are a fine example of an editorial addition. The material bearing the name of the prophet was thus preserved for future generations.

Prophecy is not exclusive to Israel. An inscription found in Syria and dating to the eighth century BC records optimistic words brought by a prophet to king Zakir of Hamat from the baal of heaven. Another inscription records an oracle of victory from the goddess Ishtar delivered by a prophet to the Assyrian king Esarhaddon in the seventh century BC. Such messages are derived from dreams or different kinds of divination, traces of which procedures are found in the Old Testament too. The phenomenon of prophecy, of people speaking for a god, is widespread, but the prophets of Israel speak from their faith in the God of Israel, whose covenant with the people has profound implications for their lives. The preaching of the prophets of Israel is a most powerful and relevant part of the Old Testament scriptures. While the historical books gave interpretations of events and saw God guiding the history of the nations, the words of the prophets challenged and encouraged the people of their time with words which have an enduring relevance.

Amos the herdsman

The earliest of the prophets now known as 'writing prophets' probably wrote nothing. He was a herdsman of Tekoa, south of Jerusalem, who felt an irresistible call to travel to the northern kingdom of Israel during the reign of king Jeroboam II to deliver words of Yahweh. The time of Jeroboam II, who reigned from 783 to 743, was a period of prosperity for many, but not for all. A time of peace allowed trade to flourish and the population to increase. But while some prospered, others were deprived.

Covenant ideals reflected in the Pentateuch and in the book of Joshua established a vision of a society of equals. Every Israelite was to have access to the necessities of life. Each one was to possess a portion of land and those in greatest need were to receive the assistance of the stronger ones. This vision of a just society began to be undermined once the monarchy was established. Solomon imposed taxation and forced labour which led to different levels of society. As the kings of Judah and Israel came and went the situation did not improve. The rich could usurp the property of the poor, as Ahab usurped Naboth's vineyard. The rich of Amos' day ignored the covenant obligations towards the poor. This realisation and zeal for the covenant drove the herdsman of Tekoa to speak out.

We know very little of Amos and of the circumstances of his call. What we do know is that the call from Yahweh was irresistible. 'The Lord Yahweh speaks: who can refuse to prophesy?' (Amos 3:8) Yet Amos does not claim any status as a prophet. A narrative of Amos' ministry is inserted somewhat awkwardly in 7:10-17. The prophet has been preaching at Bethel, one of the two sanctuaries established two hundred years earlier for the kingdom of Israel by Jeroboam I. At Bethel Amos is challenged by Amaziah, priest of Bethel, who sends Amos back to the kingdom of Judah. Amos replies, 'I am not a prophet, nor am I a member of the sons of the prophets. I am a herdsman and I look after sycamores' (7:14). He adds: 'Yahweh took me from the herds and Yahweh said to me, Go and prophesy to my people Israel' (7:15). The story establishes that to speak for God it is not necessary to be a professional prophet or to be a member of a prophetic guild or union. A herdsman going about his daily work can hear the voice of God. A peasant who cultivates sycamore figs to feed to his animals can have his life dramatically altered by God. The freedom of Amos from earthly authorities allows him to challenge political and religious leaders in a foreign kingdom.

The book of Amos begins with a collection of oracles against foreign nations. Several writing prophets have such speeches attributed to them. The universal domain of the God of Israel is hereby suggested. The oracles illustrate that Israel and Judah are not alone in deserving the critical voice of the prophet. The collection of oracles against Damascus, Gaza, Tyre, Edom, Ammon, Moab, Judah and Israel shows signs of compilation over a long period. The oracle against Edom comes from later times, for it recalls how Edom 'pursued his brother with the sword' (1:11). The Edomites, traditionally descended from Jacob's brother Esau, took advantage of the destruction of Jerusalem and the deportation of the people at the hands of the Babylonians in 587 BC, well after the time of the prophet Amos.

The final oracle, against the northern kingdom of Israel, seems to introduce us to the style and content of the authentic Amos. This extended speech in 2:6-16 itemises some of the violations of the covenant now widespread among the people of Israel. 'They have sold the just man for silver, and the poor man for a pair of sandals' (2:6). The selling into slavery of the just man suggests corrupt judges, who take bribes to condemn the innocent. The poor man, on the other hand, is forced to sell his own person and become a debt-slave, when he owes only an insignificant debt, the price of a pair of sandals. People are becoming slaves for insignificant reasons. The covenant law did allow for slavery, which was widely accepted in those times, but all Israelite slaves were to be freed after six years in the sabbatical year (Exodus 21:2). There is reference too in this speech to the abuse of a young girl by both a father and his son. Perhaps the ill-treatment of a slave-girl is meant. Others have retained the cloaks taken as pledges from poor people as guarantees of repayment, another deed outlawed in the covenant code (Exodus 22:25/22:26). These actions highlight the plight of the poor and vulnerable. Those singled out for protection in the social legislation of Israel have become the victims of the selfishness of the new rich of Israel in Amos' day. Parallels with contemporary society do not need to be spelt out.

The speech continues with God's recollection of mighty deeds wrought for Israel: the exodus and the gift of the land (2:10). Punishment is threatened, in which none of the proud warriors of the kingdom of Israel will escape. This first lengthy speech against social abuses in Israel has been placed with the other oracles against the nations, but it is clearly a major example of the words which Amos had the courage to declare beyond the border in the northern kingdom.

The words of Amos can be striking and dramatic. 'You alone have I known of all the tribes of the earth,' says Yahweh, alluding again to the special relationship of God to Israel. The restatement of this relationship would seem to put Israel at ease, but Yahweh adds, 'therefore for all your sins will I punish you' (3:2). At another point the Israelites who might survive punishment are compared to 'a couple of legs, or a bit of an ear' salvaged by the shepherd from an attacking lion's mouth (3:12).

Social oppression is accompanied by an extravagant lifestyle for the rich, but their houses of ivory and houses of ebony will be pulled down by Yahweh (3:15). A famous judgement speech is delivered against the 'cows of Bashan', the women who spend their days in luxury and drunkenness. Bashan was noted for its rich pastureland. Cows will be treated as cows, and Amos describes how they will be driven off towards Mount Hermon and deportation (4:1-3). A further speech refers to other luxuries: ivory beds and divans, lamb and veal, harps and other musical instruments, wine and oil. 'But they do not care about the ruin of Joseph,' the speech ends (6:6). 'Joseph' is used frequently among the prophets to refer to the northern kingdom, for the tribes of Manasseh and Ephraim, the two sons of Joseph, occupied a large amount of its territory. The words of Amos are as relevant today as they were then. They can be applied to any society where the vulnerable are exploited, and they have relevance to the contemporary world situation when rich nations lack sufficient political courage to alleviate the poverty of the poor.

The oppression of their fellows and consequent extravagant style of life makes the people blind to their religious hypocrisy. They use their beliefs to support their complacency, and this complacency Amos challenges. To those who consider Yahweh looks benignly upon them and that the day of Yahweh will be a day of light, Amos presents a vision of a day of darkness (5:20). An exasperated Yahweh rails against Israel: 'I hate and despise your festivals' (5:21). 'Spare me the din of your chanting' (5:23). Yahweh requires justice, not extravagant liturgies. This theme recurs frequently among later prophets, as in Isaiah 58:1-8. Liturgy where there is no justice and truth undermines itself. Amos even has Yahweh attack the very idea of a chosen people: 'Are not you and the Ethiopians the same to me, Israelites? It is Yahweh who speaks. Did I not bring Israel out of the land of Egypt, the Philistines from Caphtor, and the Arameans from Kir?' (9:7) This bold questioning of Israel's status as the people of God is brought about by Amos' indignation at Israel's religious complacency.

The patience of God is, it seems, exhausted. At one point Amos mentions Yahweh's repeated attempts to cajole Israel into a change of behaviour. Famine, drought, locusts, death by disease and sword, natural disaster, none of these is sufficient to bring Israel back to Yahweh (4:6-12).

A set of five visions provided for the prophet by God appears in Amos chapters 7-9. When Amos has a vision of locusts about to devastate the land, his pleading brings about God's change of heart. The same occurs in the second vision when drought is threatened. Once the third vision comes, God's decision is firm. God will use a plumb-line to test the uprightness of the people. The decision to destroy is irrevocable. A fourth vision employs a play on the Hebrew word qets, which means 'the end'. Amos is shown a basket of ripe fruit, qayits in Hebrew, for the time of the end, qets, has arrived. The final vision shows Yahweh on the point of ordering that all be punished. Wherever they may try to hide, Yahweh's justice will find them (9:2-4).

It seems therefore that the message of Amos is one of total destruction. God's patience has been exhausted. There is no way forward for the people but the way of punishment. There are however traces of hope, though these are very reduced. 'Seek me and you shall live,' says Yahweh in 5:4. Is this a long-since disregarded invitation from the prophet? Further limited hope is expressed in other texts (5:14-15 and 9:8) but these seem to be additions to the genuine message of the prophet. The final verses of the book (9:11-15) are clearly the addition of an editor from later times. They allude to Jerusalem's destruction and to the survival of the land of Edom after attacks. Similarity with the text of Joel 4:18-21 also speaks for these verses being material from after the exile. The Old Testament scholar, Julius Wellhausen, once referred to these concluding verses of Amos as 'roses and lavender, instead of blood and iron'.

It seems reasonable to conclude that Amos had despaired of the future of the people of the northern kingdom. Their disregard for the social consequences of the covenant and their neglect of true religious commitment left the prophet with no other message but the announcement of a stark future. It is not surprising that when the book was written down other writers added some more hopeful

statements. Yahweh condemns injustice unequivocally. But forgiveness is also part of Israel's faith, as the prophet Hosea will
amply show.

Hosea and the vulnerability of God

The two minor prophets who spoke their words to the people of the
northern kingdom complement each other. While Amos trenchantly
expresses the punishment due to those who disregard the covenant
stipulations, Hosea attempts to understand the inner feelings of the
heart of God. Hosea uses human emotion to speak of God's being
torn between love and hatred, between tenderness and violence.

There are signs in the book of Hosea that this prophet was active
after Amos, when on the international scene Israel and other neighbouring kingdoms began to be threatened by the resurgence of the
Assyrians, the great power to the north. Under the leadership of
Tiglath Pileser III, known in the Old Testament as Pul, Assyria
imposes its rule over the region. During the reign of king Menahem
Israel accepts the status of vassal to the Assyrians. Menahem pays
extensive tribute in order to maintain his hold on power in the
northern kingdom (2 Kings 15:19). The annals of Tiglath Pileser
give independent testimony that 'Menahem of Samaria' paid tribute to the Assyrian king.

Stability is not achieved. Israel is tempted to form alliances
against Assyria both with its small northern neighbour Syria and
with Egypt, the great power to the south. And the kingly office is
frequently threatened by coups in the northern kingdom, as 2 Kings
chapter 15 makes clear. After the death of Jeroboam II six kings
reign in approximately twenty years. Zechariah reigns for six
months before being murdered by Shallum, who in turn is murdered by Menahem. Menahem was succeeded by his son, Pekahiah,
who reigned for two years before falling victim to a coup engin-
eered by Pekah. The final king of Israel, Hoshea, removed Pekah
and plotted an alliance with Egypt. Tiglath Pileser's successor
Shalmaneser then intervenes. He besieges Samaria and deports the
Israelites to Assyria. The northern kingdom comes to an end in 721
BC. These traumatic events are the backcloth to Hosea's preaching.

Much of Hosea's preaching is concerned not with international affairs but with Israel's religious attitudes. Since earliest times Israel's religion has had to contend with the presence of Canaanite forms of worship, which from time to time were adopted by the Israelites. The book of Judges testifies to worship of pagan gods at the time of Israel's settlement. It is clear from the book of Hosea that attempts, like those of Elijah, to purify religious worship in Israel were not completely successful.

In order to confront the pagan religious practices the prophet refers to his own marriage with an unfaithful wife. As was shown in the case of Ahijah of Shiloh and will be seen in the major prophets with some frequency, it was a prophetic custom to resort to symbolic actions, to perform actions which would attract attention so that a point could be made to the witnesses. In Hosea's case his married life is a symbol for the people of Yahweh's love for unfaithful Israel. The first words of God to Hosea, as reported in Hosea 1:2, are 'Go, take for yourself a prostitute and have children by a prostitute, for the land is prostituting itself away from Yahweh.' There are many who consider that the reference to the marriage is purely fictitious. In their view there is something unworthy in a prophet consorting with a prostitute. But prophetic symbolic actions are not imaginary actions. They arise from the ancient origins of prophetic activity and they are acted out. Furthermore, the deep emotion which the prophet utilises in order to speak of the inner feelings of Yahweh suggests a real emotional struggle in his own life too. As Hosea has struggled with his love for Gomer the unfaithful wife, so he maintains has Yahweh been torn in different directions by deeply felt love for Israel.

Hosea has three children from Gomer and their names are symbolic. A son is named 'Jezreel', the name of the place where the royal house of Omri ended in a bloodbath (2 Kings 9). This son recalls Israel's violent history. A daughter is called 'not pitied', for Yahweh will no longer pity Israel. A second son is named 'not my people', for Yahweh resolves to disown Israel. Yahweh's struggle is symbolised when later on this son is renamed 'my people', and the daughter 'pitied'. Yahweh is torn between rejection and love.

Hosea illustrates how Israel has been unfaithful by worshipping

Baal. The worship of Baal involves offering sacrifices on the high places, the shrines of the local gods (4:13). They have also resorted to fertility rites in which ritual prostitution was practised to ensure fertility in animals and fertile land. Hosea also upbraids the Israelites for their worship of the bull. He refers to the 'calf' of *beth-'awen*, the 'house of wickedness', in order to ridicule the bull statue set up by Jeroboam I in the shrine at Bethel, the 'house of God'. Just as Gomer has prostituted herself with other lovers than Hosea, so has Israel sought other gods than Yahweh.

Further infidelity is seen in Israel's political manoevring. Hosea describes Israel as 'a silly, witless pigeon, calling on Egypt, and going after Assyria' (7:11). She makes a treaty with Assyria, and oil is sent to Egypt (12:2/12:1). The alliance with the Assyrians is not approved. The attempts to make alliances with other nations such as the Egyptians are approved even less. Hosea sees this as the latest stage in Israel's history of infidelity, which reached a previous high-point with the setting up of the monarchy, the crime committed at Gilgal (9:15). Israel surely deserves the punishment of annihilation for all these infidelities, both religious and political.

Yet, the God of Hosea is not the God of Amos. It is true that this prophet can use violent imagery for God. 'I will be like a lion to them, like a leopard lurking on the road. Like a bear robbed of cubs I will attack, I will tear the flesh round their hearts. The dogs shall devour them, the wild beasts shall tear them to pieces' (13:7-8). But Yahweh also expresses determination not to give rein to such fierce anger. 'I will not give way to the heat of my anger, for I am God, not a man' (11:9). Hosea shows God recalling the love felt for Israel in its young days in Egypt. Despite their infidelities, Yahweh has remained faithful. The tender expressions of God's love are accompanied by disappointment at Israel's straying off to false gods. The final chapter of the book depicts the healing and forgiveness of Yahweh. 'I will love them freely' (14:5). 'They will return to live in my shade' (14:8).

Hosea makes the point that Israel's history with God is not finished. The God who is outraged by Israel's infidelities is the God who loves Israel tenderly. The prophet does not give a final answer.

He cannot foresee what will happen to the relationship between God and God's people. He speaks from his own experience of human love and expresses the dilemma and the vulnerability of God. Hosea is the first to use the symbolism of marriage in reference to the relationship between God and Israel. Later and greater prophets, such as Jeremiah and Ezekiel, will develop the image in their different ways. Hosea's contribution to developing ideas of God in the Old Testament is rich and profound.

CHAPTER 8

Isaiah and Micah

While kings came and went in the northern kingdom and this kingdom moved slowly towards catastrophe, a succession of kings
passed down power in the davidic dynasty of the southern kingdom of Judah. Since the division of the kingdom after the death of
Solomon, the southern kingdom had enjoyed more stability than its
northern neighbour, despite repeated hostilities between Judah
and Israel. In the eighth century BC stability and prosperity are
established in both Israel and Judah. The long reign of Jeroboam II
in the northern kingdom, during which Amos launched his criti-
cisms of Israelite society, corresponds to the equally long reign of
Uzziah in the southern kingdom of Judah. Due to Uzziah's leprosy
his son Jotham ruled the country. It is in the year of Uzziah's death
that the great Jerusalem prophet Isaiah is recorded as having heard
the call to prophesy in the temple in Jerusalem. Having overcome
his terror at the awe-inspiring vision he says: 'Here I am. Send me!'
(Isaiah 6:8).

A book of many prophets
The book of Isaiah is the longest of all the books of the Old
Testament, containing a total of sixty-six chapters. At first sight it
appears that all this material belongs to the prophet Isaiah of
Jerusalem, who lived in the eighth century BC. The title at the start
of the book proclaims it to be 'the vision of Isaiah son of Amoz concerning Judah and Jerusalem, which he saw in the reigns of Uzziah,
Jotham, Ahaz and Hezekiah, kings of Judah'. Closer inspection,
however, leads the reader to question whether this title is appropriate for the whole of the book of Isaiah.

The book of the prophet Amos has already demonstrated that

100

such a collection of prophetic speeches may well come from several sources. The final verses of Amos clearly belong to a much later time than that of Amos himself. On a much larger scale it is apparent that several people from different times contributed to the sixty-six chapters of the book of the prophet Isaiah. Prophetic material is intended for the contemporaries of the prophet. Once it is written down it can be preserved for future generations, but the primary intention of any prophet is to speak to the people of his own day. Kings of eighth century Judah, such as Ahaz and Hezekiah, and problems experienced in their time, such as the consequences of Assyrian dominance in the region, are mentioned at various points in the first thirty-nine chapters of the book. Ahaz has an encounter with the prophet Isaiah in chapter 7. Chapters 36-39, largely copied from the second book of Kings, concern the invasion of the Assyrian king Sennacherib during the reign of Ahaz's son, Hezekiah. The issue of Judah's relationship with Assyria and other kingdoms in the vicinity is raised in many of the chapters preceding Isaiah 40. In other words, the indications are that Isaiah 1-39 contain a considerable amount of material from the life-time of Isaiah of Jerusalem.

Once the reader embarks on Isaiah chapter 40 a new world and a new era is apparent. The few historical references from this point on are to events of the sixth century. The people of Judah have suffered deportation to Babylon. Their return to Judah is to come about due to the rise of the Persian king Cyrus, who has brought Babylonian dominion to an end. The issues raised from Isaiah 40 onward are those of the return from exile in Babylon. The God of Israel is both able and willing to restore the people to their own land. God will use Cyrus the Persian to accomplish this. Judah's relationship to the Assyrian power is long since forgotten.

Since we are dealing with some material from the eighth century BC and other material from the exilic period in the sixth century BC, it is not surprising that different literary styles also emerge. At the beginning of Isaiah chapter 40 the challenging tone of Isaiah of Jerusalem gives way to the warm and consoling style of the prophet of the exile. The content also changes. While Isaiah of Jerusalem

stresses the need for conversion and the necessity to trust in the
God who made a commitment to the davidic dynasty, the exilic
prophet stresses that the God of Israel will indeed deliver the people from a seemingly hopeless situation in a far-away land.

The book of Isaiah can be seen to contain two main parts, with
two major prophets as contributors. But the composition of the
book of Isaiah is yet more complex than this. A further division of
chapters is generally accepted which considers the material in
Isaiah 56-66 to belong to the period of resettlement in Judah after
the exile and to be a compilation of writings from a number of individuals. Thus scholars speak of First (Proto-) Isaiah, Second
(Deutero-) Isaiah and Third (Trito-) Isaiah. Furthermore, several
individuals seem to have contributed to the material in Isaiah 1-39.
The material most likely to belong to the time of Isaiah of Jerusalem
is to be found in chapters 1-12 and 28-32. Isaiah 24-27 contains apocalyptic material, which may well deserve the latest date of all the
material in the whole book of Isaiah. In order to focus on the words
of the prophet who experienced God's call in the temple in
Jerusalem in the year of the death of king Uzziah of Judah, we need
to look more closely at Isaiah 1-12 and Isaiah 28-32, as well as considering Isaiah 36-39, the chapters copied from the second book of
Kings.

More on social justice
The prominence of Isaiah's political preaching often leads to excessive concentration on the issue of trusting in God rather than in
political alliances, the question raised already by Hosea's accusations to the northern kingdom of 'political adultery'. Much attention is also given in Christian tradition to the texts concerned with a
future ideal king. But Isaiah also has much to say concerning social
conditions. This material is to be found principally in the first five
chapters. Many scholars consider this to be the earliest stage of the
preaching of the prophet, before he became involved in advising
the kings of Judah on matters of international relations.

After the initial title of the book in 1:1 there is a call to attend a
legal hearing. Heaven and earth are summoned to hear Yahweh's

accusations that despite God's care the people have rebelled. They lack knowledge and understanding (1:3). The people of Judah and Jerusalem are compared to those of Sodom and Gomorrah. They are practically as bad, though Yahweh has not destroyed them completely (1:9).

Then God launches into a speech concerning the hypocrisy of the religious observance of those who do evil and disregard the claims of justice. Amos chapter 5 presented similar accusations against the people of the north. As Yahweh hated their feasts and chanting (Amos 5:21-23), so here Yahweh rejects sacrifices, holocausts, liturgies, assemblies, pilgrimages and prayers (1:11-15). All these are rendered unacceptable by the sin of the worshippers. Yahweh has other priorities: 'Learn to do good, seek justice, help the oppressed, be just to the orphan, defend the widow' (1:17). A possibility of conversion is envisaged. Scarlet sins can be made white as snow. Conversion, return to Yahweh, is the prophet's primary concern.

A lament is then sung for the city of Jerusalem, the faithful city which has become a harlot, the city which now has lost all justice, but the lament suggests the possibility of conversion. The city will be purified and become again a city of justice, a faithful city (1:26). The famous oracle of the mountain of the temple of the Lord and its exaltation above all others follows. All nations will ascend to it to receive the teaching of God. This poem, in Isaiah 2:1-5, is repeated in Micah 4:1-3. It seems to originate among the poems of Isaiah of Jerusalem which stress the status of the city and idealise the anointed king of Judah. The vision of Isaiah, that 'they will hammer swords into ploughshares and spears into sickles', remains a powerful hope for the world even today.

The principal intention of these early chapters, however, remains that of calling people to conversion. God is against all human pride and every kind of injustice. Isaiah's God has a deep longing for justice, which is expressed in the song of the vineyard in Isaiah 5:1-7. The prophet introduces the song with the words, 'Let me sing for my friend a song of his love for his vineyard.' A story is told of the friend's attentive care for his vineyard, as he dug it, cleared it of

stones, planted choice vines, provided it with tower and wine-press
and then waited expectantly. The vine yields only sour, unusable
grapes. The prophet then has God speak, and God, who is now seen
to be the friend, asks the people to deliver a judgement. God
announces the vineyard's imminent destruction, for 'the vineyard
of the Lord of hosts is the house of Israel, and the men of Judah are
that chosen plant.' God has lavished care on the vineyard which is
the people, but has not received the desired fruit. The text ends with
a play on two Hebrew words. Instead of 'justice' (*mishpat*), there
was 'bloodshed' (*mispah*). In place of 'righteousness' (*tsedaqah*),
there was nothing but 'cries of distress' (*tse'aqah*). This song is a
parable designed to make the culprits admit their own guilt. It is
like the prophet Nathan's parable of the poor man's ewe lamb told
to David in 2 Samuel chapter 12. The song of the vineyard emphasises God's waiting, waiting for good grapes, waiting for justice and
righteousness. The prophet shows God to be still waiting for the
good fruits expected from such attentive care. Other prophets, such
as Jeremiah and Ezekiel, will take up again the theme of the people
as the vineyard of God. The waiting God who longs for the free
response of free human beings is a fundamental feature of Jewish
and Christian theology.

Trust in God

Isaiah's message of conversion to the God who requires justice and
righteousness invites the people to refocus their lives and conduct
on their God. They are in short to trust in God. Such trust has implications not only for social relationships, but also for political issues.
Trust in God implies not only fidelity to the laws of God but also
reliance on God. In the political crises of his day Isaiah stresses that
reliance on God is crucial.

   In the early years of Isaiah's prophetic career the northern kingdom of Israel had already become vassal to the Assyrian king
Tiglath-Pileser III, known in the Old Testament as 'Pul'. Some years
later they formed an alliance with their northern neighbour, the
Arameans, and planned resistance to Assyrian rule. Part of their
plan was to force the kingdom of Judah into the anti-Assyrian pact.

The narrative of these events is found in 2 Kings chapter 16 and in Isaiah chapter 7. The kings of Israel and Aram besiege Jerusalem in order to force Ahaz of Judah to join their anti-Assyrian alliance. Isaiah 7 gives the story of the encounter of the prophet with the king.

Isaiah is accompanied by his son Shear-yashub, whose name means 'a remnant will return'. This name suggests the limited response of the people to God's call to conversion. The prophet meets Ahaz as the king seems to be ensuring water supplies for the threatened city. Isaiah tells the king to have no fear of the neighbouring kingdoms, implying that Judah and its king have God's protection. The final words of the prophet are most significant. He urges the king to trust: 'if you do not trust, you will not stand firm.' This second half of verse 9 contains two forms of the Hebrew verb 'aman. The word has many connotations, but fundamental to it is the notion of support. A more literal translation can reveal the play on the word 'aman by the prophet: 'if you do not accept the support (of God), you will not be supported'. The prophet urges the king to put trust in God first. If Ahaz trusts in God, relies on God and believes in God, he will receive whatever help he needs. Nathan had spoken of God's support to king David using the same Hebrew word: 'your house will be supported for ever' (2 Samuel 7:16). To acknowledge God as the fundamental support, the crucial presence in life, has wide-ranging repercussions. For Ahaz a God-centred life would make demands on him as king.

A second speech of Isaiah follows, beginning in Isaiah 7:10. The speech, which contains the celebrated prophecy of the Immanuel, has a complex history of interpretation in Judaism and Christianity. It is important to understand its original setting and meaning. Isaiah makes a second attempt to persuade the king to trust in God. A reading of 2 Kings 16 reveals why the prophet may have felt it necessary to address a second speech to the king. In that chapter Ahaz solves the crisis brought on him by the approach of the hostile kings by appealing for help to Tiglath Pileser III, and offering to become his vassal. We do not know at what point in the crisis the prophet may have delivered his words to Ahaz. Had Ahaz already sent off his message to the Assyrian king? Was it simply a danger that Isaiah foresaw? In this second speech Isaiah seems to lose patience with Ahaz. He proposes that the king ask for a sign from God, but this is sanctimoniously refused. Isaiah nevertheless announces an imminent sign: 'the woman is with child, and will give birth to a son, and will call him Immanuel' (7:14). The famous Immanuel prophecy can be understood from the context of 2 Kings 16 and Isaiah 7. The birth of a son is the sign God gives to Ahaz, for the woman is most likely to be the king's wife. The birth of a son will be the birth of an heir, a future king of the dynasty of David. The sign therefore confirms God's promise to David, that his dynasty is supported by God. Such a child demonstrates what his suggested name, Immanuel, states: God is with the people. If God is with the king, there is no need to fear. The trust of Ahaz would be justified.

The speeches in Isaiah 7 suggest that Ahaz doubts God's support. Isaiah loses patience with a king who seems unwilling to trust in God. In the event Ahaz becomes vassal to the Assyrian king by sending his message 'I am your servant and your son' (2 Kings 16:7). The anointed king of Judah, the descendant of David, known traditionally as son of God (2 Samuel 7:14), volunteers to become son of the Assyrian king. 2 Kings 16 tells of the consequences of Judah's new status as vassal: tribute is to be paid and Assyrian religious practices infiltrate. Some have asked whether perhaps Isaiah was rather naïve in his advice to Ahaz. Was his advice simply: trust in God and all will be well? Or was the prophet perhaps more subtle than he is considered by some commentators? For Isaiah trust in God is acceptance that God is the fundamental support of all that exists and in particular of human beings and their affairs. The king is faced with a difficult decision, but without trust in God he will remain unsupported. Perhaps the prophet's enthusiasm needed to be curbed by the king's realism, but the enduring word of the prophet to all who listen is to recognise God as the source and support of life.

The prophet's message of trust to Ahaz seems to go unheeded, but his conviction does not wane. During the reign of the son of

Ahaz, Hezekiah, the prophet continues to urge trust in God and reprimands politicians for their double-dealing. Once Judah has become vassal to Assyria the temptation to seek assistance from Egypt is always present. The prophet is particularly scathing about the secret dealings of the rulers of Judah who claim they have come to terms even with death and with Sheol, the abode of the dead (28:15). Once again the prophet uses the Hebrew verb 'aman to affirm that the one who trusts has no cause for fear (28:16). No good will come from seeking the aid of Egypt, for Egypt always disappoints expectations (30:7). The people will be saved through conversion and tranquillity; their strength is to be found in quietness and trust (30:15).

The question of trust is raised for a final time in the chapters borrowed from the second book of Kings. Hezekiah joins a revolt of other kings against the Assyrians on the death of the Assyrian king Sargon II. It is the notorious Sennacherib who punishes those who have revolted. Details of the siege of Jerusalem in 701 BC can be found in Sennacherib's own report of his campaigns. He boasts that he made Hezekiah a prisoner in his own city 'like a bird in a cage'. Isaiah chapter 36 and 2 Kings chapter 18 report the mocking speech of an Assyrian official at the walls of Jerusalem. 'In whom have you put your trust?' taunts the official. He undermines the little trust the people may still have in Hezekiah and in God. Once again the prophet is the teacher of trust in God. For God says: 'I will defend this city and save it, for my sake and for the sake of my servant David' (37:35). The story tells how the city survives due to God's protection.

Future trust

The tradition of God's promise of solidarity with David and his descendants is cherished and reaffirmed by the prophet Isaiah. The kings of Judah and the city of God survive. Both Ahaz and Hezekiah survive their crises. Isaiah's dealings with Hezekiah even include the healing of an ulcer which seemed to threaten his life (38:21). But the prophet also expresses hope for an ideal future king. Both prophets and psalmists begin to present portrayals of a new

David, a king as none has yet been. These so-called messianic prophecies are an expression of hope, hope that God who cares for Israel will raise up a worthy ruler for the people.

Two celebrated poems of Isaiah express the nation's desire for an ideal king. The poem in Isaiah chapter 9 begins: 'The people that walked in darkness have seen a great light; on those who live in the land of the shadow of death a light has shone.' Three reasons for thanksgiving and rejoicing are announced. There is to be an end to oppression. There is to be an end to warfare. A child is to be born. The birth of a royal son is the greatest reason for rejoicing and hope. As the birth of Hezekiah showed that God was with the people, so does the birth of this ideal king. The king is virtually God's viceroy.

In a fashion similar to that used for the coronation of Egyptian pharaohs, this new king is awarded royal titles. He is celebrated as 'wonder-counsellor', for wonders are expected of him as they are of God. 'Warrior God' is his second title, a rare use of the Hebrew word 'el in reference to the king. 'Father of all time' speaks of the ideal of endless reign for the king. 'Prince of peace' suggests the desired harmony of the reign of the ideal king. The fundamental character-istic of this king's reign will be the presence of those qualities deeply desired by God but not found in God's vineyard, the quali-ties of justice and righteousness. It is finally made clear that Yahweh's jealous love will bring all this about. This first poem of the messiah stresses the yearning for peace and justice, a desire which it seems was not satisfied during Isaiah's days. The birth of the son to Ahaz did indeed demonstrate that God was with the peo-ple, but the hopes associated by the prophet with the coming of the ideal king were to remain unfulfilled.

A second poem of the ideal king can be found in Isaiah chapter 11: 'A shoot springs from Jesse.' The preceding verses, the last of chapter ten, described Yahweh as cutting down the heights of the proudest trees, symbols of political and military might. By contrast, the humble shoot of the stock of Jesse, father of David, is allowed to prosper. Yahweh has power to destroy the nations, but cares for the davidic dynasty. The spirit of the Lord rests on this shoot of Jesse, 'a spirit of wisdom and insight, a spirit of counsel and power, a spirit of knowledge and the fear of the Lord' (11:2). As the crowned king in Isaiah 9 was given royal titles, the king here receives the fulness of God's gifts. The spirit given to judges and kings is to remain with the ideal king. The gifts are those associated with the idealised figure of king Solomon.

The gifts of the spirit allow the ideal king to judge justly (11:3-4). He has a particular concern for the wretched and the poor. Just as the social legislation of Israel and the social concern of earlier prophets had special regard for the disadvantaged, so now the ideal ruler is seen to make the marginalised his first priority. The Old Testament thus presents a constant challenge for individuals and societies to redress unjust social conditions. The ideal king wears a loincloth of righteousness and a belt of trustworthiness (11:5). The Hebrew word for this last quality, *'emunah*, is related to the verb *'aman*. God's trustworthiness is reflected in the behaviour of God's representative.

A final section of this poem extends the vision to include the transformation of creation. 'The wolf lives with the lamb, the panther lies down with the kid' (11:6). The peace of the reign of the ideal king is not simply an end to war, but entails the re-establishment of harmony among all living things. It is a vision of paradise restored. The harmony of Genesis chapter 2 is re-established. Some scholars have considered this to be Isaiah's final poem. It expresses a hope beyond the healing of the ills of one society and beyond the pacification of international relations to speak of a healing of universal ills and reconciliation among all living creatures. Such healing, Isaiah maintains, comes from the knowledge of God (11:9). Isaiah the prophet speaks of God's plan for the world. Despite his lack of success as a prophet, presented as God's will in the story of his call in 6:9-10, Isaiah trusts the trustworthy God and is confident that future generations will see the fulfilment of the plan of God.

Micah of Moresheth

The greatness of Isaiah of Jerusalem in his poetic style and in his statements about God has rather eclipsed his contemporary, the prophet Micah. Very little is known of this prophet, except that he was from Moresheth, about twenty-five miles south-west of Jerusalem. The title of the book which bears his name states that he heard the word of God during the reigns of Jotham, Ahaz and Hezekiah. At a time when Isaiah preached in Jerusalem, Micah it seems proclaimed the word in the countryside of Judah.

The title of his book also states that he had 'visions of Samaria and Jerusalem'. The prophetic careers of both Isaiah and Micah witness the last years of the northern kingdom and the destruction of its capital Samaria in 721 BC. While Isaiah's preaching is focused on the social and political problems of Judah and Jerusalem, the material in the book of Micah concerns both the northern and the southern kingdoms. This has led some scholars to suggest the book is the work of two separate prophets, one active in Israel and one in Judah. Others consider that some of the more optimistic sections should be attributed to a 'second Micah'. What is undeniable is that the book alternates between judgement and salvation. Accusations and judgement in the first three chapters give way to optimistic speeches in Micah 4-5. Micah 6-7 begin with more accusations, while the final verses express hope for the future. By comparison to the book of Isaiah, the case for a second prophetic figure behind the book of Micah is rather weak, but such an explanation cannot be ruled out.

The book of Micah gives two fine examples of what is known as the 'prophetic law-suit', an example of which was seen in Isaiah chapter 1. In these texts God is presented as bringing legal accusations against the people. In 1:2 all the peoples and the whole earth are called to witness, and in 6:1 the mountains and hills are summoned to hear the accusations. In similar fashion to Amos and Isaiah, Micah brings accusations against the rich, who take over the property of others (2:2) and drive women and children from their homes (2:9). Rulers are accused of devouring people, tearing off skin and crushing bones (3:3). Micah also attacks the false prophets who proclaim peace to earn more money (3:5). Corruption of princes, priests and prophets is rife (3:11).

Among the speeches proclaiming a brighter future we find once more Isaiah's poem of the coming of the people to the mountain of the temple to receive God's teaching. This poem from Isaiah chapter 2 is repeated in Micah chapter 4. For Micah, as for Isaiah, God's promise to David and God's choice of Jerusalem are fundamental. Micah also speaks of a future king who will bring security. He is to be born in Bethlehem, city of David: 'but you Bethlehem-Ephrathah, least of the clans of Judah, out of you there will come for me the one who is to rule over Israel' (5:1/5:2). As with the Immanuel prophecy of Isaiah, a time of distress will lead to a time of peace and security. This ruler will feed the flock like a shepherd. His reign will bring *shalom*, the peace in which all is as it should be.

Perhaps the most momentous of the sayings of the prophet is found within the law-suit in chapter 6. Yahweh has brought complaints against the people, reminding them of many deeds in their history. A repentant people then asks what kind of sacrifice would make appropriate amends. They even entertain the possibility that only sacrifice of their children would suffice. Yahweh's reply leaves no doubt that what is required is not sacrificial rituals, but conversion which touches the person's whole way of living: 'He has told you, man, what is good. What Yahweh asks of you is to do justice, to love fidelity, and to go humbly with your God' (6:8). This verse has been described as a one-verse summary of the whole of the Old Testament law. The verse declares that the actions of every person must be acts of justice (in Hebrew *mishpat*). Every person is to acknowledge the worth of every other and of all God's creation. It states that every person is called 'to love fidelity'. 'Fidelity' or 'faithful kindness' (in Hebrew *hesed*) is a fundamental attitude of God, to be imitated by God's people. The verse speaks finally of 'walking humbly with God'. Only human beings walk with God, but they do so in awe as cherished creatures.

Both Isaiah and Micah affirmed the place of God as the focus of the trust and motivation of each person and of the whole people. These prophets urged their listeners to walk with God and to practise justice and kindness. The words they left us are equally relevant as people of today continue to search for fundamental values and wisdom for living. There is ever a need for justice, faithful kindness and for walking humbly in awareness of God.

CHAPTER 9

Jeremiah and the last kings of Judah

Dark days come as the reign of Manasseh, son of Hezekiah, begins. A much later tradition even suggests that this evil king had the prophet Isaiah executed by being sawn in half. The sins of Manasseh, who reigned for more than forty years, are seen as the cause of God's punishment in later years (2 Kings 23:26-27, 24:3). Judah remains vassal to Assyria, which reaches the height of its power in the seventh century BC and extends its empire as far as the Egyptian city of Thebes. But Assyria's days were numbered, and Judah, its kings and its prophets would be seriously affected by the consequences of Assyria's fall.

Jeremiah and king Josiah
Manasseh is succeeded by his son Amon, who is removed from power after only two years. The next to reign is the young Josiah, who becomes king at eight years old. Josiah will reign for thirty-one years (c. 640-609), though initially power is in the hands of his protectors. He is remembered as doing what pleases Yahweh and famous for his religious reform. His reign sees the beginning of the ministry of Jeremiah the prophet, who will speak for God during the most traumatic period of the history of Judah. In the early period of his ministry, Jeremiah's contemporary Zephaniah also assumes the role of prophet.

In the style of earlier prophets, Zephaniah brings words of judgement to the people of Judah due to worship of false gods and social oppression. He focuses on the coming 'day of Yahweh', the day of judgement of which Amos and Isaiah also gave dire warnings. Zephaniah's forthright words on the day inspired the Christian hymn *Dies irae*: 'a day of wrath, that day, a day of distress and anguish, a day of ruin and devastation, a day of darkness and gloom, a day of cloud and blackness' (1:15). Zephaniah speaks not only of trouble coming to Jerusalem, but also of the threat to the Assyrian capital Nineveh. The final sections of this short prophetic book provide more positive material. A 'humble and lowly people' will survive (3:12). Yahweh will live among them and renew them. It seems that the book of Zephaniah may have undergone more positive additions by later editors to balance the bleak words about the day of the Lord.

The young Jeremiah is also critical of the abuses which had been practised during the long reign of Manasseh. The title to this book of fifty-two chapters suggests he began to prophesy about the year 630 BC. The story of his call in chapter 1 sees him reply to God's choice with the words 'Oh, Lord Yahweh, I do not know how to speak, for I am only a boy' (1:6). With God's strength he nevertheless begins his work as a prophet. The people have deserted Yahweh their God. The vine of Yahweh has given a poor harvest. Israel has again pursued the baals and worshipped them. The same imagery of the unfaithful wife which was so prominent in the words of Hosea reappears in Jeremiah chapters 2-3. Jeremiah speaks ominously of an enemy from the north who will devastate the land. Like Amos and Hosea, he sees God at work to punish sinful Israel through the military onslaught of their enemies.

The years of kingship of the adult Josiah are, however, not a time of insecurity. The power of Assyria wanes and Josiah is able to establish authority over parts of the territory of the extinct northern kingdom of Israel. His authority is exercised above all in a religious reform which takes place primarily in Jerusalem but extends its influence even to the sanctuaries of the old northern kingdom. King Hezekiah had attempted a reformation of worship but the effects of this reform were soon undermined during the long reign of Manasseh. Josiah's intentions to purify worship in his kingdom are encouraged by the discovery of a 'book of the law'.

The story of Josiah in 2 Kings chapter 22 narrates that Josiah had already begun to have the temple in Jerusalem repaired. It was during this work that a hidden book of the law was discovered. The

book is read out in the king's presence and Josiah tears his robes as
a sign of repentance that the laws laid down in the book have not
been observed. Subsequently he initiates a reform which entails the
destruction of all forms of pagan worship and, most importantly,
the centralisation of all sacrificial worship at the temple in
Jerusalem. This is a political statement as well as a religious move
for it includes the removal of any forms of Assyrian religious worship allowed under Manasseh. Assyria is weak enough to be tested
by confident vassals. Similarities have been detected between the
measures taken by Josiah and legislation in the central chapters of
the book of Deuteronomy. This has led to the suggestion that the
book found hidden in the temple was some early form of
Deuteronomy. Did the book of Deuteronomy, or the section known
as the 'deuteronomic code' in chapters 12-26, thus provide the pro-
gramme for Josiah's reform? How old was this material? Had it perhaps been brought south to Jerusalem after the destruction of the
northern kingdom and concealed due to the religious situation of
the reign of Manasseh? Some have suggested the book was compiled during Josiah's time, presented as speeches of Moses made
before he died, and used to give authority to the king's religious
reform.

Josiah's religious reform and his exercise of authority beyond
the borders of his own kingdom of Judah were made possible by
the decline of Assyria. Ten years after the religious reform the
Assyrian capital fell to the Babylonians in 612 BC. Having been subjects of the Assyrian empire, the Babylonians now take advantage
of its weakness and the city of Nineveh falls. The prophet Nahum,
another of the twelve minor prophets, delivers an oracle against the
Assyrian capital at about this time. Nahum uses vivid descriptive
poetry to proclaim the fall of Nineveh. He concludes: 'All who hear
news of you clap their hands at your fall. For who has not felt your
unrelenting cruelty?' (Nahum 3:19)

The rise of Babylon and its victory at Nineveh provoke the
interference of a resurgent Egypt. The pharaoh, Necho II, drives
northwards to block Babylon's advance. Josiah determines to
oppose the Egyptian invasion of his territory and seeks to obstruct

the progress of the Egyptian troops at Megiddo. Josiah is unsuccessful and dies at Megiddo. Egypt takes control in Judah and
imposes Jehoiakim, a younger son of Josiah, as a puppet vassal
king. The high hopes of Judah's independence are shattered at the
death of good king Josiah. Dark days come upon the kingdom once
again.

Little is known of the activity of Jeremiah during the reign of
Josiah. The early preaching belongs to this period, and is largely
concerned with denouncing pagan religious practices. It is evident
that Jeremiah would have supported Josiah's abolition of these
practices. Jeremiah indeed refers to Josiah as an exemplary king,
who 'practised justice and righteousness' (22:15).

Jeremiah and king Jehoiakim

At the beginning of the reign of Jehoiakim, Jeremiah delivers his
famous temple sermon. Reports of this are found in chapter 7 and
chapter 26, which exemplifies the lack of order in the book as a
whole. The prophet's message is that trust in the temple is insuffi-
cient. If people do not amend their ways Yahweh will allow both
temple and city to be destroyed. 'I will make this temple like Shiloh,
and make this city a curse for all the nations of the earth' (26:6).
There is a striking contrast here with the words of the prophet
Isaiah. For Isaiah the temple and city were inviolable. God had
made a promise to David, and would stand by it. For Jeremiah
God's justice may actually require action against both temple and
city. Both prophets attempt to explain the events of history as
directly willed by God. As long as Jerusalem survives this can be
understood as being due to God's promise of solidarity. Once its
destruction is envisaged this must surely be due to the evil deeds of
the people who are no longer worthy of the promise.

Views of how God acts in history have developed considerably
among believers. God is no longer seen as raising up rulers to act
according to God's plans. When a city lives in prosperity this cannot be considered as necessarily due to the virtue of its inhabitants.
When a place is destroyed the wickedness of its people is not necessarily the cause. As the Old Testament progresses it becomes clear

that the suffering of an individual or of a group is not necessarily brought about by their wickedness. Jeremiah's view that destruction by an alien people is God's punishment does not, however, invalidate his preaching. His enduring message has much in common with earlier prophets, as he maintains that lip-service to a religious faith without goodness of life is detrimental to people and not pleasing to God.

Jeremiah's speech brings about an angry reaction from priests, prophets and people. Does he not deserve to die for speaking against God's temple? Jeremiah 26:20 recalls another prophet, Uriah by name. Uriah had been arrested and put to death by king Jehoiakim for preaching about the destruction of the city. The crowds are divided concerning what Jeremiah's fate should be, and he has a protector, Ahikam son of Shaphan (26:24).

It seems that Jeremiah's words in his temple speech may have been brought about partly by the renewal of pagan practices in the reign of Jehoiakim. Jeremiah delivers a stern judgement on Jehoiakim as being quite unlike his father Josiah. Concerned only for his own interests, this king quite possibly allowed the religious reforms of Josiah to be reversed. Jeremiah mocks Jehoiakim by considering him worthy of a 'donkey's funeral' (22:19).

The reign of Jehoiakim is marked too by significant developments on the international scene. Egypt's control of Judah lasts for only four years. Nebuchadnezzar, the crown prince soon to become the new king of Babylon, defeats the Egyptians at Carchemish in 605 BC. Judah and its king now fall under the control of Babylon. For Jeremiah, Nebuchadnezzar is the agent of punishment brought by Yahweh against the people. Jeremiah can now be considered not only as undermining faith in God's protection of the temple and the city, but also as a traitor in league with the enemy.

Jeremiah's view of Nebuchadnezzar is reported in chapter 25. This is one of many speeches of the prophet presented in prose rather than poetic form. This may be material reworked by those who compiled the record of Jeremiah's preaching. The speech is dated to the fourth year of the reign of king Jehoiakim, the first year of Nebuchadnezzar. The enemy from the north is Nebuchadnezzar, referred to here by God as 'king of Babylon, my servant' (25:9). Jeremiah's message is clear. For failure to listen to the prophets and amend their conduct, the people must now face the invasion of Nebuchadnezzar. The prophet continues: 'I will bring an end for them to the voice of rejoicing and the voice of gladness, to the voice of the bridegroom and the voice of the bride, to the sound of the millstone and the light of the lamp' (25:10).

Needless to say, Jeremiah's preaching was unwelcome to Jehoiakim. A long narrative in chapter 36 illustrates the king's reaction to the prophetic word. Jeremiah's assistant Baruch writes the prophetic message down on a scroll at the dictation of Jeremiah. Baruch's scroll eventually falls into the hands of Jehoiakim, who destroys it by burning it piece by piece as it is read to him. Jeremiah's response on hearing about the fate of the scroll is to have all the words written down again, with many similar words in addition (36:32). As for Jehoiakim, he and his house will be singled out for special punishment on the day of disaster.

Jeremiah's preaching encourages a docile attitude to the Babylonian overlords who have won control in the region. The wisdom of such a course of action is not understood by Jehoiakim, who takes advantage of a temporary weakness of Babylon to make a reckless claim at independence by withholding tribute. Once this has been done, the return of Nebuchadnezzar to punish Judah becomes inevitable. The Babylonian chronicle of Nebuchadnezzar's reign and the second book of Kings concur that the king laid siege to Jerusalem and took it, that he appointed a new king of his own choice, and that he carried away great amounts of booty to Babylon. 2 Kings chapter 24 also informs us that Jehoiakim died during this period to be succeeded by his eighteen-year-old son Jehoiachin.

The punishment inflicted by Nebuchadnezzar is deportation of the new king and his family, the nobles, the blacksmiths and metal workers to exile in Babylon. He removed the treasures of both the temple and the royal palace. He appointed Jehoiachin's uncle, Zedekiah, as king. Thus in the year 597 this first deportation takes place. It is seen by the writer of 2 Kings, as indeed by Jeremiah, as God's punishment for the nation's sins.

Babylon has not yet finished with Jerusalem, as the story will reveal. But another prophetic contemporary of Jeremiah delivers at about this time a fierce condemnation of nations such as Babylon. They may be called by God to inflict punishment, but this nation has transgressed all limits. The words of this minor prophet, Habakkuk by name, question the view that Babylon was simply the agent of God. Judah may have deserved punishment, but Babylon is more reprehensible due to her excessive behaviour. Habakkuk challenges God with the question: 'Why are you silent while the wicked devour those who are more righteous?' (1:13) The answer given to the prophet suggests patience is necessary, and he further declares: 'the upright one will live by faithfulness' (2:4). This text is familiar to Christians due to its use by the apostle Paul when he writes about faith. Habakkuk challenges the view that the Babylonians are simply servants of God engaged in the work of punishing a disobedient nation. Some sections of the book of Jeremiah too will speak of God's displeasure at the excesses of Babylon (25:12, 51:36-37).

Between the deportations

With Jehoiakim dead, and his son Jehoiachin deported to Babylon as king of Judah, Zedekiah takes over an unenviable position at a critical time. Zedekiah comes across as a well-intentioned man who is unable to assert authority over those who have claimed positions of power after the first deportation. Jeremiah continues to proclaim that Nebuchadnezzar, the servant of God, has received from God authority over the nations (27:6). The prophet urges the king, the priests and all the people to submit to the yoke of the king of Babylon.

We are told in chapter 28 that Jeremiah's view was not held by other prophets. Hananiah the prophet, known only from this incident in the book of Jeremiah, gives the contradictory message that God has broken the yoke of the king of Babylon, and that the return of the king of Judah, of the exiles and of the temple treasures will take place after two years. Jeremiah's advice to the exiles, in a letter reported in chapter 29, is that only after seventy years will the exiles return. The yoke which Jeremiah wears to symbolise Babylonian dominion is publicly removed and broken by Hananiah. Jeremiah, accusing Hananiah of falsity, announces his imminent death. As in earlier times, there is a contrast here between prophets who preach words to please people, and those who, like Jeremiah, have the courage to speak the truth as they see it no matter what the consequences may be. The issue of how to discern the true prophet from the false one is ever present.

The reign of Zedekiah sees further ill-treatment of the prophet. Threatened with death and beaten during the reign of Jehoiakim, Jeremiah is arrested and detained under Zedekiah. Zedekiah has been driven to rebel against Babylon, presumably by withholding tribute, by the nationalistic fervour of leaders among the people and by hopes of Egyptian intervention under the new pharaoh, Hophra. Babylonian troops surround Jerusalem for the second time in ten years. Jeremiah is imprisoned on accusation of attempting desertion to the Babylonians, but Zedekiah reduces his sentence to detention in the Court of the Guard. Jeremiah was to be given a loaf of bread each day 'as long as bread was available in the city' (37:21). The strong men of the city prevail on the king to punish Jeremiah more severely. Jeremiah is lowered into a storage well where he sinks into the mud (38:6).

The physical sufferings of Jeremiah are accompanied by intense emotional suffering. At various points in the book his personal outpourings concerning his call and his fate are reported in poems known as his 'confessions'. Jeremiah speaks of those who persecute him and describes himself as 'a trustful lamb being led to slaughter' (11:19). Jeremiah complains that his prophetic calling has brought him grief but God renews the call (15:19). The third confession seeks vengeance on the prophet's persecutors (17:18), and the fourth extends such desire for punishment to the persecutors' families (18:21-23). The fifth confession is the most anguished, as the prophet accuses God of seducing him: 'You have seduced me, Yahweh, and I have let myself be seduced' (20:7). Whenever the prophet struggled to suppress the prophetic word he experienced a fire in his heart, imprisoned in his bones (20:9). The confessions of

Jeremiah contain strong emotional attacks on persecutors and angry language directed at God. Their enduring relevance is that they suggest honest emotional outpouring of feelings is an acceptable part of prayer. They make us aware of the challenge and pain involved in honestly speaking the word of God whether in prophecy or preaching. The response of God is to understand and to encourage perseverance. Nevertheless, the final section of the fifth confession ends on a despairing note (20:18).

Jeremiah is rescued from the storage well by the court eunuch, Ebed-melech, and returned to the Court of the Guard. The siege of Jerusalem, the second in ten years, lasts for eighteen months. Neither the historical material in the second book of Kings nor the reports in the book of Jeremiah provide much detail of this period. It is to the book of Lamentations that we must turn to learn something of the anguish of the doomed city. This book, which is placed after the book of Jeremiah in Christian bibles due to an ancient attribution to the prophet Jeremiah in the second book of Chronicles (35:25), contains five lengthy laments probably from different writers, concerning the siege and subsequent destruction of the royal city. Four of the poems are designed as acrostics, alphabetical poems in which each stanza begins with a subsequent letter of the Hebrew alphabet. They present the complete range of human suffering brought about by war. Infants plead with their mothers for bread. Women eat the children they had nursed in their arms. Young and old lie dying in the streets. The poet weeps ceaselessly at the pain of the people. They are unrecognisable, as the skin shrinks to their bones. The fall of the city brings the final horrors of rape and slaughter. 'Look, Yahweh, and see,' cries another poet, 'whom have you ever treated like this?' (2:20) The poems struggle too with the reason for such terrible pain. Has God done this to the people? A faint glimmer of hope struggles amid the gloom: the favours of Yahweh are not all past (3:22). The anguish of the last days of Jerusalem recalls the anguish of cities, peoples and nations since time began. People still struggle with the reason for the immense sufferings individuals and groups are allowed to endure. Faith in God is often lost amid such a struggle. The Old Testament reflects the turmoil in people's minds when they seek reasons for such suffering. It will be for the book of Job to place such questions in the wider context of the freedom God bestows on all creation, a freedom God will not violate nor take back. The gift of making free decisions, given to human beings, is of immense worth and of immense consequence.

The second book of Kings reports the ending of the siege in chapter 25. Zedekiah is captured, forced to witness the execution of his sons, blinded and taken to Babylon. Temple, royal palace and all the houses of Jerusalem are burned. What remains of the population is deported to Babylon, though the poorest are left to work the land. Jeremiah is not harmed. No doubt the Babylonians were aware of his activity.

Hopes for the future

Jeremiah lived through the most dramatic period in the history of Judah. He preached the word during the reign of several kings, as the situation of the kingdom went from bad to worse, from difficult to desperate. His task was to interpret events, to decipher what was God's word for the people. During repeated tragedies Jeremiah also keeps alive hopes for the future which are recorded in the section starting in chapter 30. The material here may originally have looked forward to the restoration of the northern kingdom of Israel. Rachel, the matriarch of the north, is told to cease her weeping and dry her eyes (31:16). Much of the material here has been edited to make Judah as well as Israel the recipient of these words of future hope.

The most notable of the oracles in this section announces the establishment by God of a new covenant. The people have broken the covenant made when they left Egypt. The new covenant is to be different: 'I will place my law within them, I will write it on their hearts' (31:33). This text envisages a radical change in the understanding of the law. People will accept it as their own, as part of them. A radical conversion is envisaged. Jeremiah heralds here the new tone which will be found in the prophets of the exile, who will speak about the future after the disaster of Jerusalem. Ezekiel and

the Second Isaiah will speak in their own ways of these new beginnings. Jeremiah's text concerning the new covenant was taken up
by Christian writers as a way of understanding the new time
brought by Jesus of Nazareth. A further text in 31:38-40 speaks of
the rebuilding of Jerusalem and its consecration to Yahweh, another
theme vigorously developed by the prophets of the exile, Ezekiel
and the Second Isaiah.

Jeremiah refers just once to the coming of a new king, a righteous branch for David who will exercise justice and righteousness
in the land. This text in 23:5-6 is found repeated in 33:15-16. Its
brevity and similarity to the more extensive messianic material
found in the first part of the book of Isaiah suggest that the messianic
hope was only a minor component in the prophet's hopes for the
future. Perhaps kingship was not willed by God after all.

Jeremiah would not live to see his hopes fulfilled. He was con-
vinced that the future of the people of God lay with those who had
been dragged off to Babylon. They were the good figs which he saw
in a vision shortly after the first deportation (24:1-10). He was confident that in time they would return. But Jeremiah himself was
forced to go with Baruch to Egypt where it seems he ended his days
(43:6-7). The focus of attention in the unfolding story of the people
of Judah now moves to the land of Babylon.

CHAPTER 10

Ezekiel and the Second Isaiah

In two successive waves the people of Judah were deported to the land of Babylon. In the first deportation the young king Jehoiachin, members of the royal family, the nobles and the blacksmiths were exiled. Ten years later the new leaders and the common people were transported, leaving only the poorest in the land. Riches of palace and temple had been pillaged. City and temple lay in ruins. Thousands had died by famine and war. Over and above the death and destruction, the survivors were traumatised. How could this happen? How could God allow this? As so often in the histories of peoples, at Amritsar and Auschwitz, in Cambodia and Rwanda, they could find no satisfactory answer. Added to this came the physical separation from the land of their birth. They were desolate and destitute in a distant pagan land. Where was God now?

The Old Testament contains written record of the words of two prophets of the exile, both of whom attempted to answer the questions of these survivors and to console them in their anguish. These prophets, Ezekiel and the anonymous prophet we call the Second Isaiah, spoke of the future where there was no future, of hope where there was despair, of new beginnings where the end had come.

Ezekiel and the exile
The opening verses of the book of the prophet Ezekiel testify that this prophet was among those exiled with king Jehoiachin in 597 BC. The editors of the book occasionally give dates to introduce prophetic visions and speeches. The earliest date is found in chapter 1, and refers to the fifth day of the fourth month of the fifth year of exile. On this day Ezekiel is reported to have seen a strange vision.

Anyone starting the book of Ezekiel might easily be put off by reading chapter 1. It provides a detailed description of a vision. Among the cloud and flashes of fire Ezekiel sees four animals, each with four faces and four wings. These four animals are provided with wheels. They seem to move by wheels and wings. A sound is heard 'like mighty waters, like the voice of Shaddai, like a storm, like the noise of an army' (1:24). Ezekiel sees a throne and one like a man seated on the throne. The whole vision is described as 'like the glory of Yahweh' (1:28). Ezekiel prostrates himself.

After this lengthy introduction and its description of 'the glory of Yahweh', a voice speaks to the prophet. God calls him as a prophet to a 'house of rebels' (2:3). He is given a scroll, which he is instructed to eat. This initial vision of Ezekiel shows the prophet receiving the word of God, but more importantly it describes the arrival of the 'glory of Yahweh' in the land of exile. The complicated imagery of chapter 1 should not obscure the message which is fundamental to the prophet's preaching. Yahweh has come to stay among the people exiled in Babylon. God's concern for them continues. God is present in Babylon. The vision of the 'glory of Yahweh' will be seen again.

Ezekiel belongs to a priestly family (1:3). He is the son of Buzi, the priest. He sees his first visions by the rivers of Babylon, by the river named Kebar. The preoccupation of the first years of his prophetic work is with the fate of Jerusalem. Those deported in the first wave are naturally anxious about the future of Jerusalem. They know the volatility of the situation and that it would take little to provoke king Nebuchadnezzar to repeat his attack on Jerusalem and its survivors.

The prophet seems well aware of the danger of another revolt against the Babylonian overlords. He uses symbolic actions to illustrate to the people the siege, the dire situation of those trapped inside the hungry city and the plight of those who flee (chapters 4-5). Ezekiel is deeply aware that the history of Israel is a history of sin. He uses parables, like that of the vine in chapter 15, and allegories, like that of the young foundling girl saved by Yahweh in chapter 16, to make the point that Judah like Israel has deserved the punishment of exile and destruction.

A further vision in chapters 8-11 describes how the prophet, transported in a vision to Jerusalem, witnesses the shameful sins of its inhabitants and looks on as the city is punished. As the doomed city comes to its end, the prophet witnesses the departure of the glory of Yahweh from the temple (10:18). God's dwelling place in Jerusalem is destroyed, but God is with the people in a far-away land. Ezekiel's awareness of what was happening in Jerusalem has led some to suggest he returned there, or left there only after the destruction. It is more plausible to consider these visions as seen from a distance and to trust the evidence of the book that Ezekiel left Jerusalem with the first deportation in 597 BC. The prophet expresses in many different ways, by vision, parable, allegory and judgement speech, that the people have deserved punishment.

The prophet can thus be seen to accept the principle that individuals and peoples bring disaster on themselves. He is nevertheless aware that such a simplistic view may be questionable. Ezekiel knows that a saying is being bandied about among the people: 'The fathers have eaten unripe grapes, but it is the children's teeth that are set on edge' (18:2). The people have implied that some are suffering without deserving it. The issue is raised that suffering does not always follow from sin. But Ezekiel upholds the principle: it is the one who sins who will die (18:4). For Ezekiel all have sinned and all have deserved God's punishment. His successor as prophet among the exiles, the one known as the Second Isaiah, will suggest that some meaning lies in undeserved suffering.

The prophet has spoken about the coming destruction of the city. As the first half of the book ends, the material concerning the time before the destruction, the prophet is told of the imminent death of his wife. He is told not to mourn for all are to suffer a grievous loss in the time ahead (24:24).

Ezekiel and future hopes

A central section of the book of Ezekiel, from chapter 25 to chapter 32, contains speeches against various nations. The prophet's words against unreliable Egypt, 'the great crocodile wallowing in his Niles' (29:3), show extraordinary imagination and vehemence. The crocodile is to be dumped in the desert with all its stinking fish. After this interlude we see a new Ezekiel emerge. The words of the prophet to those in exile can no longer be words of judgement and disaster. God has a new message. God has a future in store for them and God is able to accomplish that future. God is present with the exiles and will one day intervene.

The section of the book of Ezekiel which begins with chapter 33 contains his words of hope for the future. The fundamental statement that there is hope and that God still cares for the people is presented in many varied forms. The prophet receives a new call to prophesy. As was stated when he began his work, he is to be a watchman who warns the wicked to turn from their ways (33:7, 3:17). The despondency of the people is counteracted by the consideration that Yahweh rewards the goodness of their lives. Turning from evil and towards good will guarantee their future. While those left behind in Judah are punished, the exiled people are given hope.

One of the most extensive of the speeches of the prophet announcing new hope after judgement is contained in chapter 34. We may well have here a cluster of different speeches of the prophet and maybe of his disciples too. They all use the image of the shepherd to symbolise rulers. Ezekiel begins by delivering judgement on the shepherds of Israel who look after themselves rather than caring for the flock. 'You have fed on fat, you have dressed yourselves in wool, you have sacrificed the fattest sheep, but failed to feed the flock' (34:3). Due to poor governance the sheep have been scattered. The people have lost their home and livelihood. It is God who will now intervene to shepherd the flock (34:11). Just as the psalmist in Psalm 23 speaks of God as his shepherd, so here God adopts the whole people.

The actions of this good shepherd are the good news which is awaited by the exiles. Still using the image of the shepherd and the sheep, the prophet describes what the intervention of God will mean. Like a shepherd, God cares for the flock, keeps it in view, rescues the lost, brings the exiles home, pastures them throughout the land, feeds them in good pasturage, allows them rest, searches for the lost, brings back the stray ones, bandages the wounded and makes the weak strong. The prophet's exhaustive list of the activities of the good shepherd is an allegorical description of the healing which God is to offer to the exiles.

Later in this lengthy chapter the image of shepherd is applied to a new ruler. God promises to raise up a shepherd, 'my servant David'. This davidic ruler will be their prince (Hebrew *nasi'*). The word for 'king', *melek,* is avoided, perhaps due to the disasters experienced by Judah and Israel under the kings. New images are brought in. God will make a 'covenant of peace' with the people (34:25). The relationship between God and the people will establish harmony. They will be safe and secure in a fertile land.

Another major speech to encourage those in exile begins with Yahweh's affirmation that the intervention is intended to protect Yahweh's 'holy name'. The deportation and desperate straits of the exiles have led to contempt and mockery for the God of Israel from pagan nations. God retorts: 'I am not doing this for you, but for the sake of my holy name' (36:22). The actions of God will demonstrate God's greatness to the nations. God will gather the people together again. They will be cleansed of defilement and idols. The prophet declares that God will give a new heart and a new spirit. Inner transformation is the work of God, and leads to righteous conduct, just as Jeremiah had promised the law of God would be written on the hearts of the people (Jeremiah 31:33). The gift of the spirit to the whole people is promised again.

The spirit is at work again in the famous vision of the dry bones in chapter 37. The prophet sees a valley strewn with dry bones and in his vision God commands him to call on the spirit to come and enliven a stricken people. The vision speaks of the restoration of a people. 'We are as good as dead,' they say (37:11). But by word and vision the prophet counters their despair. As the chapter continues we come across a final symbolic action of Ezekiel. He holds two pieces of wood, one for Judah and one for the northern kingdom (37:16). He unites them as one to symbolise the hope of a united people of God. There will be one people, one king, one shepherd. An eternal covenant of peace is promised (37:26).

It can be seen how the various salvation speeches of the prophet proclaim the same hope of Yahweh's intervention. Perhaps the most puzzling of the speeches is the one concerning the imaginary enemy, Gog of Magog, in chapters 38-39. When all is fulfilled and the people of Israel dwell again in safety in their own land, it is imagined that God brings against them a mighty coalition of armies led by an enemy from the far north, Gog of Magog. The coming of Gog will be accompanied by cosmic convulsion. The earth will quake, the creatures of earth and sea will be petrified, the mountains will fall. This imaginary scenario represents the prelude to God's final intervention to overcome the enemies of God. It is an early example of apocalyptic writing, literature in which visions of the end of the world are described. Gog and his armies are destroyed, the weapons of war will be used for firewood, it will take seven months to bury the dead and cleanse the land of corpses, and birds and animals will gorge themselves on the flesh and blood of princes. The scene is indeed apocalyptic. These chapters assure Israel that God will protect the people from whatever foe comes against them.

It is not surprising that such material has been used for political purposes. At face value the text might seem to guarantee Israel's survival and to exonerate any measures taken against Israel's enemies. Ezekiel shows no concern for the conversion of the nations, but as biblical tradition develops it becomes apparent that God has a concern for all nations. The people of God are all those who seek God in truth. The enemies of the people of God are those who place obstacles on the road to peace and justice.

The final chapters of Ezekiel provide a final vision. It runs from chapter 40 to chapter 48. Ezekiel has a vision of the rebuilt temple of Jerusalem. In the vision instructions are given for its building and use. At one point Ezekiel witnesses the return of the 'glory of Yahweh' to the rebuilt temple (43:2). But the most extraordinary part of this long vision is when the prophet in chapter 47 describes the life-giving waters which flow from the temple of God. They become more and more abundant and transform the landscape from the holy city to the Dead Sea. The barren wilderness becomes verdant. The sea itself, with its putrid content of minerals, is totally changed and supports teeming life. The banks are covered with trees giving fruit each month. God's presence not only transforms the fortunes of the people and brings about their return. It also radically enlivens the landscape, bringing life in abundance where death reigned. As in the opening chapters of Genesis, God's concern is for the earth and all its creatures.

The variety and impact of the salvation oracles of Ezekiel is remarkable. Much of this material will be rediscovered in the warm poetic lines of the later exilic prophet, the anonymous one we have become accustomed to refer to as the Second Isaiah. It is perhaps appropriate to recall first the minor prophet whose book is known as the shortest of all Old Testament books. The twenty-one verses of the prophet Obadiah are largely a condemnation of the activities of Edom, Israel's sister nation, which took advantage of Jerusalem's fall to gain large parts of the territory of Judah. The enmity between the ancient ancestors of each nation, Esau and Jacob, narrated in the book of Genesis, is rekindled by this action.

Second Isaiah and the return

Anyone reading through the book of the prophet Isaiah will notice a profound change of atmosphere on reaching chapter 40. The opening words are: 'Console, console my people.' It rapidly becomes clear that these verses of encouragement are set in Babylon as the period of exile continues. 'Speak to the heart of Jerusalem, and call to her that her time of service is ended, that her guilt is atoned for, that she has received from the hand of Yahweh double punishment for all her sins' (40:2). The coming deliverance from Babylon is compared to the ancient liberation of Israel from slavery in Egypt. Just as God by tradition dried up the sea to allow the people to escape, so God will now provide water for Israel's journey through the desert to return home to Judah (43:16-21). The prophet tells the exiled people not to remember past deeds but to prepare for something quite new and unexpected.

The poems of this prophet contain significant developments in Israel's ideas of God. God is certainly a liberator. God does indeed desire the people's freedom. God is concerned that they be restored to their home. But other questions also arose from the experience of exile. Israel was without doubt exposed to Babylonian worship of gods and goddesses and perhaps came up against the cult of the Babylonian creator god, Marduk. In the ancient creation story 'Enuma elish', Marduk was portrayed as the one who vanquished the monster known as Tiamat and who created the world. It was probably in the exilic period that the priestly creation story, which eventually found its place in chapter 1 of Genesis, was written down. Like the priestly writers of the material in the book of Genesis, the prophet Second Isaiah also reflected on God as creator of all. Various references to God's activity as creator are found in 40:12-26. This God made the earth and everything on it. The prophet uses the Hebrew word for 'create', *bara'*, numerous times.

Perhaps the most challenging of all these statements comes in 45:7, where a literal translation of the Hebrew produces, 'I create good and evil.' The totality of what exists and the whole spectrum of activity and experience comes from God. It is important not to rush to the conclusion that the prophet is attributing moral evil to God. We can recall that the book of Genesis did not provide a satisfactory solution to the question of the origin of evil. In the story of the loss of the garden of Eden a talking snake played the part of the initiator of evil. If Second Isaiah is to proclaim Yahweh as greater than any foreign god, he must proclaim Yahweh the creator of all activity and experience. It will be left to the book of Job and later literature to develop further the question of the sinister origins of evil. The Hebrew term *ra'* means 'evil', 'pain', 'hurt', 'sin', and more besides. Everything which is not 'good' (Hebrew *tob*) is *ra'*. While the priestly author in Genesis 1:31 has God create everything as 'very good', Second Isaiah risks the question of the origin of the 'not good'.

If the God of Israel is the creator of all, this God has power to achieve God's purposes in history. This God has power to arrange the return of Israel to the land. This God is Israel's 'redeemer' (Hebrew *go'el*). An act of redemption originally refers to the actions of a close relative who protects the rights of another. A redeemer may perhaps buy a relative's freedom when he has been sold due to debt. Second Isaiah frequently calls God 'redeemer' (41:14, 43:14), for God raises up the Persian king Cyrus to take over the Babylonian empire and restore the exiles to their home. The policies of Cyrus towards client nations were indeed magnanimous. The book of Ezra opens with the statement that Yahweh induced Cyrus to send the exiles home, and Second Isaiah sees things in similar fashion. It is quite possible that Cyrus is the inspiration of the first of the prophet's 'songs of the servant' which is found in chapter 42. 'He does not break the crushed reed, nor quench the wavering flame' (42:3). Yahweh refers to Cyrus as 'my shepherd' (44:28). Cyrus will achieve the designs of the God of Israel by having Jerusalem and its temple rebuilt. More remarkable still is the fact that God calls Cyrus 'my messiah', 'my anointed one' (45:1). God has power over all peoples, even though they may not be aware of it (45:4).

Second Isaiah and future hopes

The focus of the later chapters of the Second Isaiah is on hopes for the rebuilding and restoration of Jerusalem. In several poems Jerusalem is personified as Sion, bride and mother. Sion's lament begins the poem in 49:14-21 with the words, 'Yahweh has abandoned me, my Lord has forgotten me.' 'Does a woman forget the baby at her breast?' comes God's reply. Yahweh emphasises that even in the shocking event of mothers failing to cherish the children of their wombs, God will never abandon the people. In a world where the shocking takes place frequently, the care of God for people is constant.

Rebuilt Sion will be staggered by the multitudes returning to live in the city. The place is too small for all the arrivals. The poem speaks too of the role of the nations, who assist the return of God's people. She who was left without children or husband is amazed at the number of her children (54:1). 'Your creator will be your husband, Yahweh of hosts is his name' (54:5). This statement recalls the motif of God's marriage to Israel first found in the prophet Hosea. Many of the themes of the other great prophets of restoration, Jeremiah and Ezekiel, recur in Second Isaiah. The desert will bloom, the population will multiply, the gift of the spirit will be bestowed and an everlasting covenant will be forged (55:3).

Second Isaiah also contributes to the development of faith statements about the God of Israel. God declares that there is no other god (44:6). The presence and power of God in the land of exile has allowed people of faith to understand that no other god exists, that Yahweh is the universal God. The prophet ridicules the work of the makers of idols. They use wood to make a fire and to bake bread, using what remains to carve an idol which they worship (44:15). The sarcastic tone of these attacks shows a confidence in the superiority of Israel's religion, in which the making of images was forbidden. The God of Israel is revealed as the only God, the God of all peoples. Outreach to the nations will increase, but will have to contend with the limiting idea of a chosen people. As early as the prophet Amos, people of faith claimed that the God of Israel was the God of all nations, but openness to such an idea grew only slowly (Amos 9:7). The book of Jonah will be a major step forward in this regard, for God loves even the Assyrians. Second Isaiah has the people of Egypt and of Ethiopia (Cush) profess faith in the one God, the God proclaimed by Israel. They say, 'With you alone is God, and there is no other except God' (45:14).

Servants of Yahweh

Up to this point we have made only a brief reference to one of the poems of Second Isaiah known as the 'songs of the servant'. The prophet often refers to Israel as the servant of God, as in 41:8. But four texts are traditionally separated and take as their theme the mission and fate of a servant of God.

The first poem, in 42:1-4, tells of a servant endowed by God with the spirit in order to bring justice (Hebrew *mishpat*) to the nations. The style of this servant is remarkably meek and humble. He does not oppress the weak, he does not 'break the crushed reed' nor 'quench the wavering flame' (42:3). His own commitment is to the pursuit of justice for the peoples. The magnanimous policies of Cyrus the Persian may have inspired such a eulogy. The second poem, in 49:1-6, has the servant declare that he was called in the womb to speak for God. In his mission he has experienced exhaustion and lack of success. The call of this prophet is renewed and extended to serve not only Israel but to be a 'light for the nations'. In 50:4-9 we first encounter the physical suffering of a servant. Called to listen for God's word and to speak as God's disciple, the servant is punished. He suffers blows, insults and spittle. But this suffering servant is strengthened by God. He does not doubt God's support.

The longest of the poems of the servant is the last, found in 52:13-53:12. This great meditation on the meaning of suffering comes in three sections. God speaks in 52:13-15. A group of people continue from 53:1 to the first half of verse 11. God then concludes the poem. Being aware who is speaking one can make better sense of the poem. God speaks of the exaltation of the servant, a servant who 'will prosper, will be lifted up, will be exalted, will rise to great heights' (52:13). But before this the servant will suffer and lose his life. The long speech of the people describes the rejection of this servant, 'a man of sorrows, familiar with suffering' (53:3). The people declare that this innocent one has suffered for them. 'He was pierced through for our sins, crushed for our faults. The punishment that brings us peace lies on him, and by his wounds we are healed' (53:5). The servant goes to his punishment and death without a word. His life is given up as a sacrifice of reparation. The concept is found in the rules concerning sacrifice in Leviticus chapter 5. The sacrifice of reparation or atonement (Hebrew 'asham) is made when animal blood pays for human sin. The poem affirms that once his suffering is over he will see his heirs and lengthen his days. Some have seen here an idea of resurrection as a reward for the pains of the servant. Whatever the case may be, the giving of this innocent human life is seen as a sacrifice for the sins of others. The poem deals in an extraordinary way with the suffering of the innocent. Such suffering must have some sense.

The question of the identity of the servant or servants has led to much speculation. Jews and above all Christians have laboured over the problem. It has become normal for Christians to identify the servant as Jesus of Nazareth. The fourth poem has been extraordinarily influential in explaining the meaning of the death of Jesus.

It is certainly tempting to see connections between the poet's four portraits of servants of the Lord and known servants of God, but it is important to value the poems for what they offer: four ways of being servant, different situations in which God works through human beings for good. One servant promotes justice throughout the world. Another is a light for all nations. A third perseveres in the face of persecution. The fourth servant gives his life for others and is accepted by God. To identify these servants is to restrict the power of the poems. They represent ways of being servant for all those who seek God and seek the good of God's people. The poems are a vibrant challenge to people of all times and perhaps above all of our own day, when a thoroughly committed individual can intervene powerfully for good in the affairs of the world. Servants of God still give their lives for the good of the people. One has only to think of the lives of Oscar Romero or Mother Teresa to appreciate the abiding relevance of the servant songs of Second Isaiah.

CHAPTER 11

The chronicler's history
and the last of the prophets

The Old Testament contains two major collections of historical books. The collection known as the 'deuteronomistic history' includes the books of Joshua and Judges, the two books of Samuel and the two books of Kings. These books give the historical traditions of Israel from entry into the promised land to the destruction of Jerusalem in 587 BC. The second collection is known as the 'chronicler's history' and comprises the two books of Chronicles and the books of Ezra and Nehemiah. While the two books of Chronicles begin with a genealogy of Adam and end with the destruction of Jerusalem, the books of Ezra and Nehemiah take us further, providing some coverage of events from the first return from exile in 539 to about 400 BC.

The chronicler's history, like the deuteronomistic history, brings together traditions from various sources, but it has its own distinctive presentation of the historical traditions of Israel. It seems to have originated from priestly circles and emphasises that Israel is a worshipping community. The chronicler is preoccupied with Jerusalem, its temple and the liturgy. The two books of Chronicles make David and Solomon their champions. Any negative elements concerning these two kings, traditions known to us from the books of Samuel and Kings, such as David's adultery with Bathsheba and murder of her husband Uriah, are omitted in the books of Chronicles. For the chronicler, David is the one who gave instructions concerning the building of the temple and the organisation of the liturgy. Solomon is the builder of the temple who presides at its dedication. The chronicler does not mention the break-away of the northern kingdom and provides only the history of the kingdom of Judah, elaborating the deeds of those kings who instigated religious reforms, Hezekiah and Josiah. This emphasis on Israel as a wor-shipping community, for whom the city of Jerusalem and the tem-ple are of primary concern, continues in the books of Ezra and Nehemiah.

The dream and the reality

The prophets of the exile encouraged a lost people not to lose hope. They spoke of return, of rebuilding, of deeds of God which would surpass anything yet experienced. Cyrus the Persian king promul-gated his edict allowing the return of the exiles in 539. It is recorded at the end of the second book of Chronicles and in Ezra chapter 1 that the Jewish exiles were allowed to leave and to return to Judah. There they were to be assisted in the work of rebuilding the temple of their God. Such religious tolerance was shown by the Persians to client nations of all religions. The book of Ezra and the minor prophets Haggai and Zechariah, as well as the material found in Isaiah 56-66, reveal that there was some difference between the dream and the reality.

The book of Ezra refers briefly to Sheshbazzar, who is called 'prince of Judah' in Ezra 1:8. Sheshbazzar is entrusted by Cyrus with five thousand four hundred vessels of gold and silver, once looted from the temple in Jerusalem. It is quite possible that the nar-rative exaggerates both the lost splendour of the former temple and the conscientious magnanimity of Cyrus. The lists of people return-ing given in the books of Ezra and Nehemiah may reflect later cen-suses. Sheshbazzar is thought by historians to have led a rather small group of returnees.

The book of Ezra introduces in chapters 2-3 a new leader, Zerubbabel, a davidic prince, who is accompanied by the priest Jeshua, or Joshua. It was under these two leaders, with the support of the prophets Haggai and Zechariah, that work on the temple made progress. The returnees had encountered opposition both from the 'people of the land', those left behind in Judah during the years of the exile, and from the Samaritans, the inhabitants of the former northern kingdom of Israel. The Samaritans offer to assist in the rebuilding of the temple to the God whom they consider theirs too, but their offer is rejected (Ezra 4:1-3). Concern for religious orthodoxy and purity overrides any desire for the reconciliation of ancient differences.

Haggai and Zechariah encourage the work of rebuilding the temple. They are both active in the reign of the Persian king Darius I. The short book of Haggai dates his activity to the second year of Darius, 520 BC. The prophet confronts the people's view that the time has not yet come to rebuild the temple (1:2). Haggai reprimands them for giving more attention to building their own houses. They suffer from poor harvests and inadequate provisions. Abundance will come only when God looks on them with favour. Under the leadership of Zerubbabel and Joshua the people begin work on the temple. The book of Haggai gives prominence to Zerubbabel and seems to express some hope of independence from Persia. Yahweh will shake the heavens and the earth, overturn thrones and destroy the power of kings (2:21-22). Haggai's words reflect an optimistic view that Persian dominance would not last long. It would in fact endure for over two hundred years.

The book of Zechariah is much longer than that of Haggai, amounting to fourteen chapters. It is thought to belong to two separate periods. In the first eight chapters there are references to the rebuilding of the temple, to Zerubbabel the prince and the high priest Joshua and to the hopes they represent. The material is dated in the opening verse of the book to the reign of Darius I. The second part of the book, from chapter 9 to chapter 14, gives no dates, and does not mention the rebuilding of the temple. Differences of content and of style lead to the widespread contention that the second part of the book belongs to a 'Second Zechariah'.

The chapters belonging to the first Zechariah are dominated by visions, visions which are explained by an 'angel' or 'messenger' (Hebrew *mal'ak*). Such an individual has already been seen in the final vision of Ezekiel in chapters 40-48. He was referred to simply as 'man' (Hebrew *'ish*). These are our first encounters with the figure known as the 'interpreting angel' (Latin *angelus interpres*). This messenger appears frequently in apocalyptic visions to explain their meaning to the visionary. Such visions will return later in the book of Daniel.

Zechariah's eight visions do require explanations. He sees four horses of different colours sent out to patrol the world. They discover the world at peace (1:11). He sees four horns which symbolise worldly powers (2:2/1:19). He sees a man sent to measure the dimensions of Jerusalem. The man is pursued by an angel who declares: 'Jerusalem will remain without walls' (2:8/2:4). Sion's surprise at the large numbers of her children in the poems of Second Isaiah is echoed in this vision of unwalled Jerusalem. Yahweh further declares that God will be 'a wall of fire around her, and the glory within her' (2:9/2:5). As foreseen by Ezekiel, Yahweh's glory will return to the temple. A further vision presents the high priest Joshua exchanging his dirty clothes for splendid robes (3:4). The prophet then sees two olive trees standing by a lampstand, which represents the watchfulness of God. The olive trees are explained as 'two sons of oil' and seem to symbolise the two leaders, Zerubbabel the prince and the high priest Joshua (4:14). A vision of a flying scroll symbolises judgement on thieves and on those who swear falsely (5:4). In a further vision, a woman in a bushel measure, representing 'wickedness', is transported by women with wings to be set up in a temple in the land of Shinar, the pagan land of the tower of Babel (5:11). Lastly, Zechariah sees chariots sent out across the world. God's spirit reaches the pagans of the north (6:8).

With such visions we receive a foretaste of later apocalyptic writing. At first sight rather weird, they speak of the purification of the land, of God's care for the chosen leaders, for the chosen city and for the wider world.

First Zechariah ends with more straightforward hopes for the future. Yahweh will return to the rebuilt city. Where a people had been slaughtered, old men and old women will sit to rest, and boys and girls will play (8:4-5). Others too will come. People from other nations will seek the Lord of hosts in Jerusalem. 'Ten men of nations of every language will take a Jew by the sleeve and say: "Let us go with you, since we have heard that God is with you"' (8:23). Despite its strangeness, the preaching of first Zechariah powerfully presents a God who consistently cares for people, and whose care goes beyond the limits of one nation.

The third part of the book of Isaiah seems to belong to this period too. Some of the material in Isaiah 56-66 develops the poems of the restoration of Sion found in Second Isaiah. Third Isaiah considers the return of the people and the coming of the nations to the light of Sion: 'the riches of the sea will flow to you, the wealth of the nations will come to you; a multitude of camels will cover you, the drome-daries of Midian and Ephah; everyone in Sheba will come, they will bring gold and incense, and they will proclaim the praises of Yahweh' (60:5-6).

The hope that all nations will acknowledge the true God is developed here. But other poems in Third Isaiah express a dismal reality. There is injustice and violence. People go hungry and home-less. Isaiah chapter 58 contains a famous attack on false religion. Fasting should be accompanied by works of justice. The oppressed are to be freed, the hungry fed, the homeless housed, the naked clothed. The light of this nation will shine when provision is made for the needy. This message of the third part of the book of Isaiah is just as relevant to the nations of the world today. A nation is truly great, not when it proclaims itself great, but when its vulnerable ones are cared for.

The sixth chapter of the book of Ezra tells us that the temple was completed and dedicated and the passover celebrated. These events are dated to 515 BC. There follows then a considerable gap in our knowledge of events in the community. The work of Ezra the priest, in the second half of the fifth century, is the next theme of the book.

Ezra and Nehemiah

The second half of the fifth century sees two individuals make sig-nificant contributions to the moral and material strengthening of the Jewish community in Jerusalem. Ezra figures in the two books of Ezra and Nehemiah, while Nehemiah appears only in the book which bears his name. Ezra is a scribe and a priest, while Nehemiah is appointed governor. The most likely scenario seems that Ezra was despatched to Judah at the decree of the Persian king Artaxerxes I (Ezra 7:11). Ezra is to see that the law of the God of Israel is being heeded and to arrange sacrifices and offerings. It seems that Artaxerxes is being portrayed as a new Cyrus, anxious to respect the god of a client people. The decree of Artaxerxes is preserved in Ezra chapter 7 in the Aramaic language, which suggests authenticity since this was the international language of post-exilic times. What is certainly true is that the Persian rulers continued their policy of openness and tolerance towards the religions of their client peoples as a way of keeping the peace in their colonies.

The story of Ezra's journey from Babylon to Jerusalem is given in the first person, as if Ezra himself tells the tale. 'We arrived in Jerusalem and rested there for three days' (8:32). Sacred vessels are delivered and sacrifices are offered. The issue immediately challenging Ezra on his arrival is the practice of mixed marriages, marriages above all of Jewish men with foreign women. Though permitted in early times, such marriages had been forbidden in the legislation of Deuteronomy in order to preserve religious purity. The people resolve to send away their non-Jewish wives. The book does not report the social consequences of such action. The primary preoccupation is to preserve religious purity, but it is reported that Ezra chose helpers to consider all the cases of mixed marriages (10:16). The tension between maintaining racial and religious purity and openness to foreign influences will nevertheless remain.

Nehemiah is introduced as the story continues. This Jew in exile receives a visit from his brother in the Persian winter capital of Susa. The brother and his companions speak of their recent visit to Judah and of the dilapidated state of Jerusalem nearly a century after the first return from exile: 'the wall of Jerusalem is in ruins and its gates are burned down with fire' (Nehemiah 1:3). Nehemiah, who serves as cupbearer to king Artaxerxes, makes a request to be allowed to go to Jerusalem to see to its restoration, and is granted leave.

Significant details are given of Nehemiah's work on the wall, the assistance rendered, and the efforts of enemies of the Jews to hamper the work. Nehemiah, as governor of Judah, has the needs of the poor at heart. Those whose land and family members had been sold due to debts owed to fellow Jews have their debts cancelled. Without reference to a sabbatical year or a jubilee year, at Nehemiah's own initiative, debts are written off (5:12). Work on the walls of Jerusalem is completed to everyone's admiration (6:16).

At this point in the history Ezra makes another appearance. His public proclamation of the law of God in Nehemiah chapter 8 is the most memorable tradition about Ezra. On the basis of this tradition he became known as the father of Judaism and has been considered the final editor of the torah, the five books attributed to Moses. 'He read from it on the square before the Water Gate, from dawn until the heat of the day, in the presence of the men and women, and those who could understand, and all the people gave ear to the book of the law' (8:3). The reading of the law continues for seven days and is recorded as a celebration of the ancient Jewish feast of 'shelters' (Hebrew *sukkoth*), the feast commemorating the giving of the law to Moses (8:14).

The final chapters of the book of Nehemiah include a long historical prayer at a ceremony of atonement for foreign marriages, a ceremony of dedication for the walls of Jerusalem and details of a second mission of Nehemiah to Jerusalem. Ezra and Nehemiah are recalled as confirming the resurrected nation both religiously and politically. Ezra is remembered as firmly establishing the ancient law which the nation needed as the basis for its life decisions. Nehemiah stands for the defence of the nation against those who challenge its right to exist. In his social involvement he also represents compassion for those who experience hardship from debt and famine. Both Ezra and Nehemiah might be accused of nationalism and chauvinism. They make an essential contribution to the security of the restored nation of Judah. The openness to foreign nations dreamt of by some exilic prophets has been put aside. Some post-exilic prophets will raise the question again, but for the present Nehemiah's anxiety to build walls around Jerusalem triumphs over the vision of Zechariah that Jerusalem should remain without walls (Zechariah 2:8/2:4). An open Jerusalem as a city for people of all nations and all faiths remains a dream.

The last of the minor prophets
The post-exilic period saw not only the gradual completion of the torah, possibly under the guidance of Ezra. The final prophetic books too were being written and the collection of books of the

prophets was being completed. Ben Sira in the second century BC speaks of the 'twelve prophets', those we know as the 'minor prophets'. The last of these are the most difficult to identify and the most difficult to date.

The second part of the book of Zechariah in chapters 9 to 14 is clearly different from the work of the first Zechariah. Both chapters 9 and 12 begin with the Hebrew word *massa'*, meaning 'oracle', followed by the phrase 'the word of Yahweh'. The fact that the book of Malachi also begins in this way gives good reason for considering Second Zechariah and the book of Malachi together. But the similarities are limited. Zechariah chapter 9 is famous for its portrayal of a victorious messiah, who is nevertheless humble and rides on a donkey (9:9). The figure is reminiscent of the messiah described by the prophet Micah, the peace-loving shepherd. This messiah too will bring peace. Another verse speaks mysteriously of the mourning of the house of David for one who has been slain. They mourn for an only son, a first-born child (12:10). This happens amid what seem to be the final events of history. The enemies of Jerusalem are either conquered or reconciled. There is a sense of things being put right under God's oversight.

The book of Malachi contains reference to specific problems of the resettled community. There are six main sections, sometimes called 'disputations', each started by a statement of God or of the prophet, after which the people ask a question. The word *mal'aki* means 'my messenger'. We do not know the prophet's real name. Serious problems are considered in the disputations. Priests are accused of offering unacceptable animals as sacrifices and leading people astray in their teaching. Marriages with pagan wives are condemned, and divorce is also rejected. People have grown tired of obeying the law of God and see no point in it. Each of these conversations challenges a loss of zeal among the people. The prophet speaks of the coming of the day of Yahweh and of a messenger who prepares for the coming of God (3:1). An appendix to the book identifies the messenger as a returning Elijah, who will prepare people's hearts for God's coming. Prophecy is focusing more and more on questions about the end of the world.

Two more minor prophets remain. The book of Jonah is unique among the prophets. It contains not a collection of the speeches of a prophet, but an imaginary story of a reluctant prophet. Jonah is unwilling to travel to Nineveh, the Assyrian capital, to warn the inhabitants to change their ways. He is reluctant to announce the mercy of God to the ancient enemies of Israel. The well-known story tells of Jonah's flight westwards by sea, his being turfed overboard by the sailors to allay the wrath of God shown in a terrific storm, and his being swallowed by a great fish. God is shown to arrange things in such a way that Jonah will go to Nineveh, and will proclaim the call to conversion. The people of Nineveh change their ways, but Jonah cannot change his attitude. Their salvation produces only a sulky, petulant reaction in this rather pathetic apology for a prophet.

Jonah caricatures the attitude of those self-righteous Jews who do not consider pagans worthy of God's mercy. The book of Jonah is a product of post-exilic thought which builds on the openness to the nations strikingly found in Second Isaiah and challenges the fortress mentality found in other post-exilic material. As the Old Testament draws nearer to its close, it is not clear which attitude is prevalent. Is God the god of a limited, special people, or God of all?

The book of Joel is, like Jonah, difficult to date. It seems to share with the final chapters of Zechariah, and with Malachi to a lesser extent, a certain preoccupation with the day of Yahweh. For Joel it is a day of God's victory, but also a day of new things. The trigger for his preaching seems to have been a plague of locusts, understood as God's punishment. Indeed Yahweh is seen as leading the multitudes of insects in their invasion (2:11). After punishment and repentance a time of plenty follows. The most remarkable prophetic word of Joel is the announcement of the pouring out of the spirit on all people. 'Your sons and daughters shall prophesy, your old men shall dream dreams, your young men shall see visions' (3:1/2:28). The book ends with the punishment of the oppressors of Israel, showing a certain similarity to the end of Zechariah.

Questions of the future, the end, and God's intervention to establish justice in the world become more prominent in the final prophets. Such preoccupations will continue as the phenomenon known as apocalyptic writing emerges. The book of Daniel is the most celebrated example of apocalyptic writing in the Old Testament. Late prophecy and apocalypticism share a concern to clarify that world events are ultimately under the control of God, and that God will see the people of God rewarded and evil conquered. The abiding care of God is expressed in different ways and continues as a fundamental belief of the Jewish-Christian tradition no matter how long the history of God's involvement with people continues, and despite innumerable false predictions that that history was soon to end.

CHAPTER 12

The Psalms and the wisdom books

In the book of Psalms and the books known as 'wisdom books' we find rather different types of literature from those explored up to this point. Many of the books already investigated could be described as historical, even if in a rather broad sense. The books of the prophets in their turn could more often than not be linked to specific historical events or periods. The Psalter and the wisdom books cannot usually be connected with historical events or defined historical times. They consider human experience in its immense variety and the infinite number of predicaments that human life brings with it.

The wisdom books of the Hebrew Bible, the books of Proverbs, Job and Qoheleth, might be considered as reflections on life in all its variety, life contemplated in the presence of God and sometimes in the absence of God. The Hebrew psalms are fundamentally prayers and contain the outpourings of individuals or groups of people, in joy or hurt, in anger or fear, despair or longing, and in a variety of situations. While the wisdom books are literature for people to read or hear, the psalms are prayers directed to God, outpourings of human hearts to the Lord of all. It has been customary in the study of the psalms to categorise them into different groups. Scholars speak of different literary forms, hymns of praise and laments being the principal ones. This is useful, but should never obscure the fact that each psalm is unique and born from the specific predicament of the person who raises the prayer to God.

Prayers for all occasions
The books of psalms is considered to contain one hundred and fifty psalms. Occasionally a translator from the original Hebrew text has

complicated matters, either by fusing two psalms into one, or by dissecting one psalm into two. Such decisions have led to an uncertain numbering for many psalms. The celebrated Psalm 23 can sometimes be discovered as Psalm 22. Psalms 42 and 43 are really only one psalm. This confusion is part of life for the student of the psalms. Here the numbering of the psalms in the Hebrew Bible will be used. Verse numbers also often present problems, for the titles added to the Hebrew text of some psalms are sometimes numbered as verse one. Wherever there are discrepancies of verse numbering both references will be given. Further scrutiny of the psalter suggests that it contains various collections. The statement at the end of Psalm 72, 'here end the prayers of David, son of Jesse,' is just one indication of this. The book of psalms is in fact a compilation of collections of psalms.

The psalms arise from individual human situations, situations which are unique, but which at the same time are shared human experience. People recognise themselves and their experiences in the psalms. The situations cannot usually be linked to a named person or be given a date, but occasionally a particular time or even particular events are suggested. Some psalms allude to given events in their titles. Psalm 51 is a prayer for forgiveness which is related by its title to the sins of David. Some psalms seem to be very ancient. Psalm 29 seems to have developed from ancient pagan hymns in praise of the God of nature. A psalm such as Psalm 72, which speaks of the ideal king, will no doubt have been composed during the period when kings ruled over Israel and Judah. Psalm 137 clearly emerges from the years when the people were in exile by the rivers of Babylon. The situation is specific, but the prayer resonates for people with experiences of loss and bewilderment. Psalm 22 cannot be attributed to a named psalmist nor to a specific period, but the anguish and pain found in the opening words, 'My God, my God, why have you forsaken me?', have been a reality for men and women throughout history. Psalm 23 similarly cannot be fixed at a particular date, but its statements of trust and the feelings behind them belong to all people of faith. The exuberance of a psalm like Psalm 150 is similarly a sentiment experienced by people of all times and places.

These few examples suggest that the psalter contains prayers from a great variety of situations and from a variety of historical periods. Many psalms are traditionally attributed to king David, known as a harpist in the stories about his dealings with Saul, and remembered in later historical writings as the one who planned the temple and its liturgies. This collection of collections takes shape over many centuries, with the contributions of an unknown number of people who raised their prayer to God in a variety of circumstances. The psalter was probably completed in cultic circles by about 200 BC and the psalms have endured as a nucleus of prayer for both Jews and Christians throughout the succeeding centuries.

Psalms ancient and less ancient
Psalm 29 seems to have its origin in ancient Canaanite poetry and in the worship of a powerful god. The psalm may have been adapted from pagan usage. After a solemn and repeated invitation to praise and worship Yahweh, the poem is dominated by the words 'the voice of Yahweh' (Hebrew *qol yahweh*). The poet tries to recreate the sound of a storm with his repeated use of this phrase and similar sounds. The voice of God is heard in thunder and the power of God is revealed in the storm. The voice of Yahweh dominates the waters, shatters the cedars, sends lightning and makes the wilderness tremble. The description recalls the Exodus portrayal of God's presence on Sinai. The voice of God is heard seven times to indicate the fulness of God's power, but it is heard with no regularity. It erupts suddenly and frighteningly like thunder. The power of God is at one moment over the mighty waters of the sea, then over the heights of Lebanon, then shaking the desert of Kadesh. Yahweh is king, enthroned over the flood, enthroned for all time. This God gives the people strength and peace.

The psalm speaks of the power of the God who controls all. There is perhaps an allusion to the story of the flood in the book of Genesis, for peace follows after the waters are calmed. The psalmist evokes here the awe people feel when they witness the power that is beyond their control. This storm recalls the tempest in which Job encounters his God, the God who finally speaks to him (Job 38:1).

The voice of God here does not transmit words but inspires awe. Whoever witnesses such power is stupefied. The power of natural forces beyond the control of human beings still makes people wonder at the source of it all.

In similar fashion Psalm 93 speaks of the majesty and power of God. But in this psalm the allusion seems to be to God's domination of the waters of chaos at creation. The rivers may raise their voice and their clamour, but Yahweh reigns above the ocean, mightier than the waves of the sea. The sublime control of God over darkness, deep and wind, which Genesis chapter 1 described, is restated in Psalm 93. The fourth verse of the psalm gives a fine example of clever use of sound. Just as the English word 'rumble' imitates the sounds of rumbling, so the psalmist uses Hebrew phrases such as *mayim rabbim* (meaning 'many waters') and *'addir bammarom* (meaning 'great on high') to echo the tumult of the waters. This is the poetic device known as onomatopoeia. With their allusions to a God who is mighty over the forces of nature, Psalm 29 and Psalm 93 suggest ancient origins and connections with the hymns of neighbouring nations to their gods of nature.

By contrast, the psalms which speak of the king seem to belong to the centuries during which Judah and Israel were ruled by kings. The finest of the psalms concerning the anointed king is Psalm 72. Just like the two great messianic poems in Isaiah 9 and Isaiah 11, Psalm 72 sings of the ideal king. Just as in those poems, this king brings justice and peace. 'May he judge your people in rightness, your poor ones in justice' (72:2). The ideal of royal leadership lies not in force and oppression but in care for the vulnerable. He will free people from oppression and exploitation. His reign is a time of abundance and blessing (72:16). The nations will come to offer him gifts, the kings of Tarshish and the islands, of Sheba and Seba, representing distant peoples (72:10). This psalm is a prayer that the leader of the people will rule in such a way, bringing blessings and harmony among the nations. It may well have been part of a liturgy for the beginning of a king's reign.

Other psalms too seem to belong to similar contexts. Psalm 2 declares that the anointed king is the adopted son of God. 'You are my son. I have begotten you today' (2:7). Psalm 45 also celebrates the king but this time the occasion seems to be the royal wedding. The psalmist praises the good looks and stature of the king. In an excess of enthusiasm in verse 6 the psalmist even calls the king 'god': 'your throne, god, lasts for ever'. The king is understood, as David was, to be the adopted son of God. If he acts with integrity, the psalmist prays, he should live for ever. The second half of the wedding psalm delivers appropriate praise of the king's chosen wife. She is encouraged to forget her country of origin and her parentage, for her children are to be lords. The psalm praises leaders who allow God's purposes to be achieved. They are seen as God's gift.

A final messianic psalm may have its origins in ancient ideas of kingship. Psalm 110 speaks in cryptic form of the begetting of the king. This king sits at the right hand of Yahweh with his enemies under his feet. This king is a priest of the order of Melchizedek. That the king should occasionally take on the duties of a priest is justified by reference to this legendary ancient king of Jerusalem, who is mentioned in Genesis chapter 14. The psalm later refers to the king's violent treatment of his enemies. The verse in question is omitted when the psalm is prayed. Psalm 110 presents tricky problems of translation and interpretation.

The psalms which focus on the king were preserved to nurture hopes of right leadership even after the monarchy ended. Other psalms show clear signs of exilic and post-exilic origin. The most obvious exilic psalm is the one that begins 'By the rivers of Babylon, there we sat and wept' (Psalm 137:1). The prophet Ezekiel lived among the exiles by the river Kebar. Such a situation may well be envisaged here. As with Ezekiel's people, there is a constant preoccupation with Jerusalem, their lost city of God. They weep at the memory of Sion. Their captors mock them by requesting the songs of their homeland. They are unable to sing the songs of their God in an unclean land. Both piety and grief forbid it. Where is their God? God has surely abandoned them. They have been brought to a place where their God cannot be found. The prayer which emerges from their feelings of abandonment is one of revenge. They cry out to

God to punish Edom, for the Edomites, that sister nation of theirs, took advantage of the Babylonian attack on Jerusalem to gain territory for themselves. Their bitterest prayer is against the Babylonians themselves, those who razed city and temple to the ground and slaughtered the people of Sion. 'Blessed is the one who seizes and shatters your babies against the rock' (137:9). The sentiments voiced at the end of this community lament are hard and shocking. This verse too tends to be omitted in prayer. Its presence in the psalm should be understood not as divine sanctioning for the action it suggests, but as the uncontrollable pouring out of rage and hatred. Their absent God is the only one to whom they can cry out.

Psalm 126 by contrast recalls the end of exile and the return. 'When Yahweh brought back the exiles of Sion, we were like people in a dream' (126:1). Laughter and song take the place of weeping. Even the pagan nations recognise the deeds of God on behalf of the people. Yet the poem continues with a prayer to bring the captives back. Some have indeed returned, but others have not. There is a suggestion here of the difficult conditions of the return and the slow restoration which were narrated in the books of Ezra and Nehemiah. The return should be like torrents in the Negev, when rainstorms inundate the parched wadis. The image of life-giving waters was seen already in Ezekiel and Second Isaiah. The final image is that of a joyous return from harvest. Such a psalm shows how throughout their history this people turned to God in prayer in bad times and good.

Psalms of grief, trust and joy

Many of the psalms are voiced by one person, often in the depths of emotion. 'My God, my God, why have you forsaken me?' are the opening words of Psalm 22, perhaps the most well-known of those psalms known as individual laments. Despite his torment the psalmist receives no help. As happens in such laments, the psalmist describes his plight: 'I am a worm, not a man, scorned by men, despised by the people.' The psalmist speaks of the 'many bulls' and the 'dogs' who surround him, images of his persecutors. He describes his physical condition: he is poured away like water, his bones disjointed. He then appeals to Yahweh to save him from all these perils. Psalm 22 then takes a surprising turn as the psalmist sings God's praises for deliverance. It is a frequent feature of such individual laments that description of pain and persecution is suddenly transformed into praise of God as the deliverer. The emotion and pain of speaking of personal suffering can sometimes, as we saw in Psalm 137, lead to expressions of hatred and curses on persecutors. Psalm 69 is another extensive lament, this time including prayers for the inflicting of various ills on the enemies. The expression of such feelings of hatred in prayer once again does not bestow approval on retaliatory actions but suggests that God understands the feelings of those in pain and turmoil.

Calmer feelings are found in those psalms which express trust, of which Psalm 23 must be the most known and the most loved. 'Yahweh is my shepherd. I lack nothing.' The psalm presents two rich images of God: God is a shepherd, and God is a host. To illustrate each image two scenes are evoked: the description of the shepherd with his sheep, and the picture of a banquet. Jacob had described God as his shepherd from his birth (Genesis 48:15). The prophets had used the image to describe God's care for the people. Ezekiel in particular had listed the activities of the shepherd God in providing for the people (Ezekiel 34). Here in Psalm 23 an intimate personal relationship is evoked. The one who has God as shepherd lacks nothing. Such a person lies down in fertile pastures and enjoys rest. The shepherd God revitalises the life of the psalmist. The poet boasts of God's company in the 'valley of the shadow of death'. The rod and staff of God symbolise defence and guidance. The imagery of the shepherd thus includes provision for peaceful times and times of evil.

The poet then introduces the second image: God is the host who provides a banquet. While Ezekiel had listed more and more activities of the shepherd to speak of God's multiform care, the poet here brings on a new image to show the limitless features of God's providing. The table here is prepared for one person, as a visitor might be welcomed into the host's tent. Just as the dark valley presented no fear, so the hospitality of the host means that the enemies are no

threat. The anointing with oil is a sign of great honour, as was
bestowed on kings like Saul and David. Equal honour is shown to
all who trust, all who have discovered God as their support. The
abundance of God's gifts is symbolised by the cup which over-
flows. The banquet recalls the poem of Isaiah in which Yahweh prepares on the mountain a rich feast for all peoples, a banquet where
death will be destroyed and every tear wiped away (Isaiah 25). This
psalm applies tenderly to the individual the care of a loving God
which the prophets describe in relation to the whole people and to
the nations. The psalm ends with the psalmist accompanied by
'goodness and kindness'. They escort him on his journey for the rest
of his days. God the host provides a protective escort as the traveller continues on his way. The traveller is safe all the days of his
life. This psalm of the care of God for the one who trusts has been
prayed by believers through the centuries in any number of life situations. Its popularity at both joyful occasions and occasions of
death is no surprise. It is in life experiences that people discover
God as protector, provider and guide.

A final group of psalms gives expression to joy and thanksgiving. Among these is found the shortest of all the psalms: 'Praise
Yahweh, all nations. Extol him, all peoples. For his faithful love for
us is strong, the faithfulness of Yahweh lasts for ever' (Psalm 117).
This psalm gives us the essence of these great songs of praise. They
sometimes show very clear signs of belonging in public worship.
Many of the group of psalms known as 'songs of ascents' (Psalms
120-134) make reference to the pilgrims' journey up to Sion and to
public prayer. In Psalm 136 the community's refrain, 'for his faithful
love lasts for ever', is repeated after all twenty-six verses. This psalm
lists God's acts of creating as well as acts of salvation. Psalm 104 is a
much more extensive creation psalm. It shows similarities with an
ancient Egyptian hymn to the sun god. As with the creation stories
in Genesis there is a likelihood in this psalm of borrowing ideas from
neighbouring cultures. Several psalms provide surveys of periods of
Israel's history (Psalms 78, 105, 106). Understandably these psalms
deal principally with the earlier history, with the ancestors, with
Egypt, the exodus and the journey in the wilderness.

The psalter ends on an exuberant note in Psalm 150. Like many
hymns of praise in the psalter it begins and ends with 'Praise
Yahweh!' (Hebrew *halleluyah*). In addition the invitation to praise is
found eleven times in the body of the psalm. There is a call to praise
God in the temple and in the heavens. God is to be praised for
mighty deeds and for greatness. There is then a crescendo of musical instruments: trumpet, lyre, harp, drum, flute, strings and cymbals. The repetition of the resounding Hebrew word for cymbals
(*tseltselim*) is the final triumphant climax. 'Let everything that
breathes praise Yah!' the psalter ends.

Wise sayings and poems

Attributed like most of the wisdom books to king Solomon, the
book of Proverbs is in fact a collection of separate elements of traditional wisdom teaching. Most of the book, from chapter 10 to chapter 31, contains proverbs, usually simply of two lines of poetry.
Within these chapters are two collections specifically attributed to
Solomon. One collection (Proverbs 10-22) is entitled 'the proverbs
of Solomon', while the second (Proverbs 25-29) is called 'the
proverbs of Solomon transcribed by Hezekiah king of Judah'. But
other sections are attributed to 'the sages', and one to 'Agur, son of
Jakeh'. Most of the book of Proverbs then contains collections of
sayings from different origins. There are clear signs in chapters 22-
23 of borrowing from an Egyptian work known as the 'Wisdom of
Amenemope', which dates to before 1000 BC.

The contents of these proverbs might be described as conservative, traditional wisdom of a generally practical nature. In the style
of Hebrew poetry, some proverbs simply repeat an initial statement
in different words. Proverbs 22:1 reads: 'A good name is preferable
to great riches, graciousness to silver and gold.' Other proverbs present a contrast, often between what is just and wise and what is evil
and foolish. Proverbs 11:8 states: 'The just one is rescued from
adversity, the evil one takes his place.' Proverbs 11:19 reads in similar fashion: 'The pursuer of justice will have life, the seeker of evil
death.' Another type of proverb is the numerical proverb, which
features a chosen number, and that number plus one. Several

examples can be found in chapter 30. Proverbs 30:15b-16 reads: 'There are three things which are never satisfied, four that never say, Enough!: Sheol, the barren womb, earth which has not had enough water, fire which never says, Enough!' Such proverbs show a reflective observation of experience, the realities of nature and the realities of human life. They do not necessarily speak of God, or even of good and evil, but they demonstrate that all reality is a source of wonder to those who believe. All things can work together for good.

The first nine chapters of the book, by contrast, contain long poems, sometimes called 'instructions'. They may well be addressed by the sage to a disciple, addressed as 'my son'. A feature of these poems is the personification of wisdom, the presenting of wisdom (Hebrew *hokmah*) as a woman. This woman is contrasted with another called 'folly', who appears at the end of chapter 9, and with the 'evil woman', the seductress, whose activity is described in chapter 7. Wisdom speaks first in chapter 1, calling the ignorant to heed her words. Wisdom is not optimistic that the ignorant will listen to her. In chapter 8 Wisdom speaks of her origins before the creation (8:22-31). She recalls her delight at God's acts of creation: 'I was delighted day by day, at play before him all the time, at play in his created world, my delight with the children of man' (8:30-31). Such personification of wisdom is found in other wisdom books too. Some have suggested that the idea originated in Egyptian speculation about the order inherent in creation. As with the creation stories of Genesis, so in these reflections on wisdom, Israel was willing to listen to and learn from the wisdom of other peoples.

The book of Proverbs then presents wise teaching for life, teaching which is accepted and acceptable. This book, unlike Job and Qoheleth, presents no challenge to traditional beliefs. But it should not be less appreciated for that reason. Proverbs tells us that true wisdom is of God and that the wise person seeks this wisdom, which is often associated with the 'fear of Yahweh' (Proverbs 1:7). This is a fundamental reverence for God in all life's situations. An attitude of valuing traditional teaching, accompanied by openness to further insight, is shown in Israel's wisdom tradition. The same difficult balance has always been required by believers and seekers after truth.

The agony of Job

The book of Job is considered by many to be the finest book of the wisdom tradition. Unlike Proverbs, which ranges far and wide in its reflections on human life, the book of Job revolves around one issue, the question of human suffering. It is a difficult book to read, however, and one might often ask what the interminable speeches of the characters actually say about suffering. But it contains some of the finest poetry, rich in imagery and emotion.

The book of Job begins and ends as a story. There is a narrative introduction in chapters 1-2, and a narrative conclusion in chapter 42. Between these sections all is poetry, the extensive speeches of Job, of his friends and of Yahweh. The book opens with the presentation of its hero: 'There was a man in the land of Uz, whose name was Job. That man was perfect and righteous, fearing God and turning from evil.' Job had a large family and Job was very rich. The scene shifts to God's court, where the 'sons of God', who might be understood as God's courtiers, are in attendance. Among them is the character called 'the Satan'. This name means 'adversary' or 'accuser'. One might describe the Satan as a kind of public prosecutor in the court of God. The Satan was the one who accused Joshua the high priest in Zechariah chapter 3. The dialogue between God and Satan shows Satan undermining God's regard for Job. Job is only good because he is rewarded for his goodness. Could Job be good for no reward? What if his family and his riches were stolen from him? God allows the Satan to test Job. At the loss of his children and of his herds Job utters the famous words: 'Naked I came out from the womb of my mother. Naked I shall return. Yahweh gave and Yahweh took back. May the name of Yahweh be blessed' (1:21).

Satan has another conversation with Yahweh, who is satisfied that Job can be good for no reward. Satan plans to inflict bodily evil on Job. Satan is given leave to strike Job down with ulcers, from the soles of his feet to the crown of his head. Job is reduced to scraping himself in the ashpit. His wife challenges him: 'Curse God and die.' But Job says: 'If we accept good from God, should we not also accept evil?' (2:10) Satan has been proved wrong. The virtuous Job remains virtuous in the direst adversity.

It seems that the story is over and the wager between Satan and Yahweh has been settled. Job can be good for no reward. Human beings can be good for unselfish reasons. But a deeper question has been suggested by Job's predicament, the question of the suffering of those who do not deserve to suffer. At the end of chapter 2, as the narrative introduction comes to its end, three friends of Job arrive, Eliphaz of Teman, Bildad of Shuah and Zophar of Naamath. They come to sympathise with Job in his pain. It is they and Job who speak in the poetic dialogues which follow.

Eliphaz, Bildad and Zophar speak for the traditional idea that if Job is suffering he must have done something to deserve it. Such an idea can be found expressed succinctly in the book of Proverbs (10:29, 10:30, 11:5, 11:8), but it is the underlying theology of many parts of the Old Testament. In the historical books the sufferings of the nation are considered to be the consequence of sin. Suffering demonstrates the guilt of the victim. The three friends each speak three times, and after each of these nine speeches Job replies. They maintain that those who are virtuous do not suffer. When trouble comes to a person, it is deserved. Indeed, the victim should consider it a blessing that God chooses to correct him with suffering (5:17). Eliphaz attempts to console Job by saying: 'he wounds but he will bind the wound, he strikes, but his hands will heal' (5:18). Later, Eliphaz lists Job's suggested sins in a desperate attempt to vindicate his theology of God's retribution (22:4-11). But Job continues to maintain his innocence.

Job's speeches, both his initial speech in chapter 3, and those with which he answers all nine speeches of the friends, allow us to hear the depth of his pain, anger and confusion. His agony is exacerbated by his keen sense of his own innocence. Job stands for men and women throughout history in similar predicaments. How can God be so unjust? The book of Job faces the issue which most undermines people's faith in a loving God. His words might be compared to some of Jeremiah's confessions or to the strongest of the psalms of lament. Job curses the day of his birth, as Jeremiah had (Job 3:3, Jeremiah 20:14). He prays that God will crush him to end his misery (Job 6:9). When Job tries to rest God torments him with dreams and nightmares (7:14). He pleads with God: 'For how long will you not look away from me, and let me swallow my spittle?' (7:19) Instead, God continues to torture him (9:17, 10:17, 16:14). Human beings have but a short life, filled with sorrow, and yet God is relentless in judging them (14:1-3).

Despite all this, Job stoutly maintains his innocence. God has been pitiless against him, but he pleads in his defence. He speaks cryptically of a 'witness' (Hebrew *'ed*) who defends him. His tears plead for him (16:19-20). He trusts in a 'redeemer' (Hebrew *go'el*), the family member who defends the relation who has fallen on hard times. He knows his *go'el* is alive. He trusts in vindication (19:25). These texts present considerable difficulties of translation and interpretation. But it is clear that Job trusts despite his pain and his bewilderment.

In his final speech of this series in chapter 31 Job again declares his innocence. He gives an account of his life, of the evil he has not done and of the good he has done. The speeches of the friends have done nothing to undermine his conviction of his innocence. He demands that God hear him. If his accuser were to draft a writ against him, he would wear it proudly like a turban (31:35-36). Job has no reason to be ashamed. But before God does meet Job there is an interlude of a few chapters. Elihu, a theologian with a dogmatic hardness of heart and the arrogance of youth, is infuriated that Eliphaz, Bildad and Zophar have been unable to convince Job of his guilt and determines to succeed where they have failed. The speeches of Elihu run from chapter 32 to chapter 37. Job does not reply. Finally, from the heart of the storm, Yahweh answers Job.

Yahweh delivers the answer in two long-awaited poems in chapters 38-41. Some have wondered whether these speeches do anything at all to solve Job's problem. Such opinions seem mistaken. Yahweh speaks to Job from the storm, which recalls Moses' encounter with God on Sinai (Exodus 19) or Ezekiel's inaugural vision (Ezekiel 1:4). Both speeches begin with challenging words. God challenges Job to come out and fight (38:3, 40:7/40:2). The first speech then takes a surprising turn. God begins to question Job about the creation of the world. Was he present? Does he know how it was accomplished? Is he aware of the secrets of the stars, the light, snow and hail, lightning and thunder, rain and ice? Does he know how the different animals came about: the ibis and the cock with their foreknowledge of the Nile flood and of the dawn, the lioness and the raven with their need to provide for their young, the ways of goats, the freedom of the donkey, the wild ox, the ostrich, the horse, the eagle? What does Job know about these? God's plan was to provide the creation with a wonderful freedom. God challenges Job's right to question God's ways. There is more to reality than Job's world, than Job's pain, than Job's bewilderment. Job replies briefly to God: 'I have placed my hand over my mouth' (40:4/39:34). Like a scolded child Job speaks no more.

Yahweh's second speech follows and it is here that we come closest to the issue of undeserved evil. Yahweh challenges Job once again. The theme is that of justice. Job is challenged by God to remedy the injustice in the world: 'Do you have an arm like God's?' (40:9/40:4) If so, surely Job could bring down the proud and destroy the wicked. Job, who knows so much, must know how to remove evil and pain from the world, and God invites him to do so. God will then acknowledge his prowess. In these opening verses of the second speech we seem to consider the problem of the world's pain (40:9-14/40:4-9). The implication, however, is that Job cannot do what God challenges him to do. Job cannot, and neither will God. God has given freedom to creation, a freedom God will not retract, despite the pain such freedom brings with it. Once again we confront the issue of Genesis chapter 3. Evil (Hebrew *ra'*) enters the world from a mysterious source. The God who, according to Second Isaiah, 'creates good and evil' (Isaiah 45:7), here in Job seems to apologise that the pain of the world is an inevitable counterpart of the glorious freedom of God's creatures.

God continues with vivid poems describing the hippopotamus (Hebrew *behemoth*) and the crocodile (Hebrew *liwyatan*). What have these monsters to do with Job's problem? They too are creatures of God. In their freedom they are allowed to do as they please, to do as much damage as they like. No-one is going to control them. They can behave just as unreasonably as they wish. Once again Job is lost for words. His encounter with God has opened his eyes to the immensity of the creation. He realises that his words have not done justice to God's design (42:3).

The book of Job ends with the narrative telling of Job's restoration. In the case of Job he and his new family live happily ever after. But the poetic dialogues betray an awareness that it is not so for all those who suffer the agony of Job. The book offers some way forward in the dilemma of those who suffer beyond their limits. With the fourth poem of the servant in Second Isaiah, and perhaps originating likewise from the experience of the exile, the book of Job represents the best attempt of the Old Testament to reconcile innocent suffering with the goodness of God.

The challenge of Qoheleth

The book of Job threw down a challenge to a cherished idea of the wise men of Israel. It undermined their comfortable theology, in which God's ways could be easily explained. The book of Qoheleth, called Ecclesiastes in the Greek translation, also challenges the sages, but its challenge suggests a fundamental pointlessness to any quest for wisdom. Refreshing and yet disconcerting, the book of Qoheleth is a surprise entry in the Old Testament canon. The word *qoheleth* seems to mean a leader or speaker in the assembly. The Greek *ekklesiastes* suggests the same meaning. Like other wisdom books, Ecclesiastes is attributed to Solomon due to his reputation for wisdom. This fiction is maintained beyond the opening verse (1:12, 12:9). The book's contents and its challenging tone suggest it originated in post-exilic times when some old certainties had been overthrown.

What then does this preacher say? His theme is summarised in his favourite saying: 'vanity of vanities, all is vanity' (1:2, 12:8). He maintains that all human striving is pointless. All is supreme vanity, total vacuousness, absolute emptiness, perfect futility. His striving for wisdom, for pleasure, for wealth, all is wasted effort. He hates life, for death undermines everything (2:17). The breath of man is lost just as the breath of a dog (3:19-21). Wise and foolish, the good and the sinners, all meet the same end (9:2). All that man can do is to derive joy from life when possible (3:12-13, 8:15), and make the most of opportunities before descending to the land of death (9:10).

Qoheleth's pessimism does not destroy his faith in God, though he cannot understand the whole work of God (3:11). The wise may claim to understand, but, Qoheleth maintains, there are things beyond them (8:17). In words which recall Yahweh's words to Job, Qoheleth declares that the way of the wind, the mysteries of conception and the work of God are equally impenetrable (11:5). The extraordinary honesty of Qoheleth is a refreshing support to those who struggle to believe, reassuring them that God does not allow everything to be grasped by the human mind. Qoheleth, like Job, accepts that his experience of God must be limited. Many will be uneasy with the uncertainties and disrespect of this book. A zealous editor tried to put everything right in the penultimate verse of the book by adding: 'Fear God and keep his commandments: this is the whole of man's task.' One suspects that many Jewish and Christian preachers have tried to tone down Qoheleth in similarly inept ways over the last two thousand years.

The scepticism of Qoheleth has parallels in the ancient world. The Babylonian dialogue between a master and his slave expresses similar pessimism in a comic way. It ends with the master suggesting he kill his servant and himself, for all is comically pointless. The Egyptian poem known as 'The Sufferer and the Soul' is a dispute over suicide which dates to 2000 BC. Qoheleth never suggests suicide and despite all pointlessness is committed to getting the most from his life.

Qoheleth seems surprisingly modern, or even post-modern. Judaism and Christianity made a place for it in their scriptures, and consider it inspired. God does not welcome pretence in those who seek meaning and truth. God welcomes honesty, even the honesty of the atheist and the despairing. These words show a wisdom beyond that of the traditional teachers, beyond that of Proverbs and beyond that of the friends of Job. The book of Job and the book of Qoheleth, with their fearless questioning of traditional beliefs, are a challenging presence in the Old Testament for all seekers after truth.

The Song of Songs

'Let him kiss me with the kisses of his mouth.' This is an unexpected opening for a biblical book. The book known as 'the Song of Songs' (Hebrew *shir hashirim*) has as its theme the love of a man and a woman. The title 'Song of Songs' suggests it is to be considered the best of all songs. It is not exactly a wisdom book, but the first verse of the book attributes it to Solomon, due possibly to Solomon's reputation as lover of many women (1 Kings 11). Like the book of Qoheleth, the Song of Songs seems to belong to post-exilic times. The Song contains eight chapters of love poetry. The speakers can be identified from the content: a woman, a man and a group of people identified as 'daughters of Jerusalem' (5:8, 8:4). Translations sometimes give the identity of the speakers, but they are not identified in the original Hebrew text. A certain bashfulness about the content of the Song has led Jews and Christians to emphasise allegorical interpretations of the Song. The love of the man and the woman symbolises the love of God for the people. Such use of symbolism has already been found in the prophets. There is, however, nothing in the Song of Songs itself to suggest the writer intended such an interpretation.

The Song is clearly about love, and about the delight that the couple find in each other. The Song uses a rich variety of images to describe the physical beauty of the woman and of the man (4:1-5, 5:10-16). All this is set in idyllic surroundings. But there is also loss and longing as the couple yearn for each other's presence (3:1-4). The closest parallels to the Song have been found in ancient Egyptian love poetry. These poems too speak of longing in the absence of the loved one and delight when the absent one comes. There is no dependence on the Egyptian material, simply similarity.

The book of Proverbs may have suggested the need for such material in the Old Testament. Its description of the perfect wife in chapter 31 does not touch on physical love. It has stern warnings against the seductions of prostitutes (Proverbs 7). But in 30:19 a numerical proverb expresses wonder at 'the way of a young man with a girl'. The conservative sages too had a sense of wonder at the delights of human love. Israel had come across the misuse of sexual activity in its encounters with other nations. Prophets such as Hosea had fiercely rejected Israel's involvement in the sexual rites of the Baal cult. Nevertheless, the creation story of the Yahwist suggests Israel never lost sight of the beauty of human love (Genesis 2:23). The Song of Songs celebrates the love of the man and the woman as the creator intended it.

CHAPTER 13

The book of Daniel and the remaining writings

Persian domination of Judah, which had begun at the return of the exiles from Babylon to their home, lasted for two hundred years. It was in 333 BC that the young Alexander of Macedon won a decisive victory over the Persians and forged an empire which stretched from Greece to India and which transformed the life and culture of the peoples of the eastern Mediterranean. By this time Greek culture had already produced playwrights like Euripides and Sophocles, and the great philosophers, Socrates, Plato and Aristotle. Alexander had indeed been tutored by Aristotle. Alexander however died in 323 BC at the age of thirty-three, and at his death the empire was divided into four kingdoms. The people of Judah became part of the kingdom of Ptolemy I, who ruled from Egypt, from the city of Alexandria, which Alexander the Great had founded and where his mortal remains were buried. Another kingdom was based to the north in Syria and founded by Seleucus I.

At various points during the third century the two kingdoms of the Ptolemies and the Seleucids fought over the land which lay between them. Finally, in 197 BC, Judah became part of the Seleucid kingdom. A difficult period of its history was beginning.

Antiochus Epiphanes and the Maccabean revolt
Alexander's empire and the successive hellenistic dynasties introduced the Greek language, Greek customs and Greek religious ideas to the whole region of the eastern Mediterranean. In Alexandria, during the third century BC, the Hebrew scriptures were translated into Greek. Jewish ideas came into contact with hellenistic philosophy and religious thought. The encounter between these different cultures seems initially to have produced few problems for Judah.

The Ptolemies were interested in the land as a military and economic asset. In the first decades of Seleucid rule, however, the Hellenistic presence was to challenge the very foundations of the faith of Israel.

Persecution of Judaism began in the reign of the Seleucid king, Antiochus Epiphanes IV. His epithet *epiphanes* indicates that he considered himself a god, the manifestation of Zeus. Antiochus ruled from 175-163 BC. The two books of Maccabees, preserved in the Greek Old Testament, inform us of measures taken against Jewish religious practices and of Jewish reaction to them. These two books belong to the seven books which are preserved in the Greek Old Testament, known as the Septuagint, but were not admitted into the Hebrew canon. In addition to 1 and 2 Maccabees, the books of Judith, Tobit, Baruch, Sirach and the Wisdom of Solomon are preserved in the Greek version. Known as deutero-canonicals in Catholic circles, these books are also referred to as apocrypha. There has been long debate among Christians as to whether they should be accepted in the canon of scripture. It will become apparent from this chapter that these seven books have a significant contribution to make to the Old Testament.

The first book of Maccabees was preserved in a Greek translation from a Hebrew original, while the second book was written in Greek. 1 Maccabees gives an account of the persecution of Judaism and of the revolt led by the priest Mattathias. Three of Mattathias' five sons, Judas, Jonathan and Simon, become leaders of the Jewish resistance to the Seleucids. It is Judas who earns the name 'Maccabee', meaning 'hammer' (Hebrew *maqqabah*). The second book of Maccabees does not continue the history, but provides a collection of heroic stories from the time of Judas. In addition to plundering the temple, Antiochus' persecution involved the banning of sacrifices, violation of sabbaths and feasts, the building of shrines for idols, sacrifice of pigs and other unclean animals, and the outlawing of circumcision (1 Maccabees 1:44-51/46-53). The most grievous insult to Judaism was the erection of what the writer calls the 'abomination of desolation' (1 Maccabees 1:54/1:57). It seems this was an altar to Zeus, set up in the temple of the God of Israel. In addition to all this, books of the torah were burned. It should be borne in mind that the measures were supported by many in Jerusalem who were eager to adopt hellenistic ways. These were those who were ashamed of their religion and chose rather to build gymnasia and disguise their circumcision (1 Maccabees 1:11-15/12-16).

The revolt of Mattathias began when the king's officials gathered local people in the vicinity of Modein to offer pagan sacrifice (1 Maccabees 2). Mattathias and his sons refuse and the king's commissioner is killed. All those who are zealous for the law and those devout men known as *hasidim* join the revolt. Among those who colluded with pagan practices was the high priest Jason, who had bought the high-priesthood by a bribe to Antiochus and deposed his brother, Onias III.

Under the leadership of Judas the Jews gain control of a large part of Judah and the temple in Jerusalem can be purified and rededicated. Judas dies in battle and hostilities between the Jews and the Seleucids continue under the leadership of Jonathan, and then of Simon. Full independence for the Jews is won in 134 BC, and the Hasmonean dynasty descended from Mattathias rules for some seventy years until occupation by Rome.

The second book of Maccabees contains significant traditions about Jews martyred during the persecution. 2 Maccabees 7 gives the story of seven brothers tortured and killed before the eyes of their mother. As the mother encourages them to remain faithful they declare their faith in life beyond death (2 Maccabees 7:7-29). Other instances in the book testify to belief in the resurrection of the dead. Judas has prayers said for those slain in battle, trusting in the resurrection of the dead (2 Maccabees 12:44). The valiant Razis prays as he is hacked down that his body will be restored (2 Maccabees 14:46). The concept of Sheol, the land of death, had dominated the thought of Israel until now. A major step forward is made against the background of the Maccabean persecution. Belief in the power of God to raise the dead to new and everlasting life is affirmed both in 2 Maccabees and in the book of Daniel, one of the latest writings of the Hebrew Bible.

The book of Daniel

Daniel is a complex book. It has twelve chapters in the version found in the Hebrew Bible, but part of the text, from 2:4b-7:28, is written not in Hebrew but in Aramaic, a related language which became the common tongue in the region after the return from exile. The Septuagint has some additional material not found in the Hebrew/Aramaic Daniel: prayers of Daniel's friends in chapter 3, and additional stories of Daniel in chapters 13-14. Furthermore, most of chapters 1-6 contain stories about Daniel and his companions and their survival as deportees in the pagan land of Babylon, while chapters 7-12 contain apocalyptic visions.

The most plausible explanation for the complex final state of the book of Daniel seems to be as follows. In post-exilic times traditions grew up about a legendary Daniel, who had remained faithful to his Jewish religion in the pagan environment of Babylon under both Babylonian and Persian rulers. This Daniel was renowned, like the Joseph of Genesis, as an interpreter of dreams. In Daniel chapter 3 the story concerns three of Daniel's friends, who have been given the Babylonian names of Shadrach, Meshach, and Abednego. These friends survive the burning fiery furnace where they have been thrown after refusal to worship the golden statue of king Nebuchadnezzar. In similar fashion, in chapter 6, Daniel survives being thrown into the lions' den, a punishment inflicted during Persian times, when Daniel persists in praying to his God. Other traditions, in chapter 4 and chapter 5, tell of the punishment which eventually befalls the pagan persecutors, Nebuchadnezzar and Belshazzar.

These stories are found in the chapters in the Aramaic language. They were told to teach that fidelity to Israel's God would be rewarded. The stories may have some historical features but they are largely fictitious. These stories take on a new relevance during the reign of Antiochus Epiphanes, when Jewish religious practice is under attack. The survival of the three friends in the furnace and the escape of Daniel from the lions suggest that those who remain faithful in persecution will see God's salvation. The tales of judgement on Nebuchadnezzar and Belshazzar reassure the Jews that

Antiochus too will meet his deserved punishment. Chapters 2 and 7, the first and last of the Aramaic chapters, show awareness of the course of history from the exile until the time of the Seleucid rulers. They were clearly completed during the second century. Daniel chapter 7 deserves particular attention.

In this crucial chapter Daniel has a vision of strange beasts. He sees a lion, a bear, a leopard and a beast with ten horns. From this last beast springs a little horn, with 'eyes like human eyes, and a mouth that was full of boasting' (7:8). This beast is killed as Daniel watches, while the other beasts are deprived of their power. The climax comes when Daniel has a vision of God, described in terms reminiscent of Ezekiel chapter 1. Into the presence of the 'one of great age' comes 'one like a son of man' (Aramaic *kebar enash*) (7:13). The vision is explained by an interpreting angel, a figure we have already encountered in the visions of Zechariah. The beasts symbolised kingdoms which would rise and fall, clearly those of Babylon, the Medes and the Persians, and the Greeks. Daniel is presented as seeing all this from exilic times, but the amount of detail and the focus on the aftermath of the Greek empire betray the phenomenon known as 'prophecy after the event' (Latin *vaticinium ex eventu*). The fictitious visionary 'foresees' events which have already taken place so that when he speaks of the future his words will be trusted. The fourth beast is understood to be the empire of the Greeks, and the 'little horn' to be Antiochus Epiphanes. His end is therefore announced.

The 'one like a son of man' also represents a people. This image stands for the 'saints of the Most High' (7:22, 7:27). Those who remained faithful in the persecution of Antiochus are rewarded with sovereignty and kingship. It is important not to confuse the 'one like a son of man' in Daniel 7:13, which refers to the faithful people, with later use of 'son of man' for messianic figures. The text of Daniel was reinterpreted in this way in later centuries as messianic speculation continued.

This chapter of the book of Daniel is a fine example of an apocalyptic vision. Daniel proclaims the final triumph of God over the powers of the world. An apocalypse is a revelation and is designed to reassure people that good will ultimately triumph over evil and God over the enemies of God. It is not surprising that apocalyptic writing became popular in times of persecution. A fundamental theme in apocalyptic is that of the 'kingdom of God'. God's reign will be established and the kingdoms of the world will be subdued. Ezekiel's words on Gog of Magog (Ezekiel 38-39) and the preaching about the end found in the prophets Joel and Second Zechariah prepared for this development.

The chapters of Daniel in the Aramaic language present encouragement to those under stress and reassure them of God's assistance in times of trial, of the end in store for the persecutor, and of God's final establishment of the kingdom. Daniel chapter 1 and chapters 8-12, written in Hebrew, still need explanation. They were added in Hebrew perhaps to allow the Daniel collection easier access into the Hebrew scriptures. Chapter 1 serves to introduce Daniel and his three companions and explain how they came to be in the court of Nebuchadnezzar. The final chapters of the Hebrew/Aramaic Daniel elucidate the vision of Daniel 7. They focus on the destruction of the persecutor, the establishment of the reign of God and the resurrection of the dead. Daniel 12:2 proclaims belief in the resurrection in the following words: 'many of those who sleep in the land of dust will arise, some to eternal life, others to eternal shame and disgrace.' Daniel, like the writer of 2 Maccabees, affirms that God takes human beings beyond the grave and beyond the decay of Sheol. The questionings of the Old Testament about life beyond death are finally resolved in the apocalyptic focus on life in the kingdom. Other apocalyptic writings which did not find their way into the Old Testament, and the writings of the New Testament, will further develop Jewish and Christian ideas that God's care for human beings goes beyond physical death.

Finally, we should acknowledge other Daniel traditions found only in the Greek Bible. Chapter 13 shows the young Daniel's shrewd condemnation of two lustful old men in the story of Susanna. The story shows many traits of folk literature. More entertaining stories are to be read in Daniel chapter 14. Daniel reveals the deceit of the priests of Babylon who night by night feast on food left before the image of Bel and claim Bel does the eating. Daniel also does away with a dragon worshipped in Babylon by feeding it balls of pitch, fat and hair. A final story is a parallel to the story of Daniel in the lions' den. All these traditions celebrate the superiority of Israel's God and the wisdom and protection afforded to God's faithful.

Two Jewish heroines

Like the book of Daniel, the book of Esther belongs to the Hebrew canon, but contains additional sections only found in the Greek Septuagint. These additions to Esther amount to about one third of the text in the Greek version. The book of Esther is a disturbing tale. Though it may be related to some original historical incident it seems unlikely to be historical. Mordecai, the guardian of the orphan Esther, lives in the Persian capital of Susa during the reign of king Ahasuerus. This is the Persian king known as Xerxes, who ruled from 486 to 465 BC. This same Mordecai is described as being one of those deported from Jerusalem with king Jehoiachin in 597 BC (Esther 2:6). Such inconsistency demonstrates from the start the fictitious nature of the story.

The story opens with the drunken king summoning his queen Vashti in order to display her to his banqueting companions. Vashti bravely refuses and is deprived of her royal status. Mordecai enters Esther in the contest for Vashti's replacement, warning her to conceal her Jewish identity. Esther of course wins the contest. Mordecai, who is a government official, meanwhile learns of a plot against the king and is able to warn him by informing Esther. The villain of the story, the notorious Haman, is also introduced at this point. On the promotion of Haman to high rank in the king's service, Mordecai refuses to bow before him. Haman plots not only the murder of Mordecai but also the extermination of all Jews in the Persian empire. The king issues an irrevocable edict to this effect.

The Greek additions to Esther contain a prayer of Mordecai and a prayer of Esther. In his prayer Mordecai explains that his refusal to bow to Haman, which has generated such dangerous hatred of

the whole Jewish race in such a powerful official, was for good reason, for Mordecai will bow to God alone (4:17e/13:14). Esther's
prayer is one of the finest in the Old Testament. She prepares to go
to the king unsummoned, a deed punishable by death. Fear and
courage are combined in her heartfelt words (4:17l/14:3-4). When
Esther enters the king's presence, he is moved to treat her kindly
and Esther asks that Ahasuerus and Haman attend a banquet she
prepares. On the second day of the banquet Esther pleads for her
people and turns the king against Haman. Haman is hanged without delay on the towering gallows he had prepared for Mordecai.

Up to this point the story seems innocent enough. An evil
schemer has come to an evil end through the courage of Esther. A
new decree is issued by the king which allows the Jews to take any
measures in self-defence against any attacks on them. The story
reports that five hundred enemies of the Jews were killed in Susa,
and also the ten sons of Haman at the special request of Esther. The
Jews throughout the empire slaughter seventy-five thousand of
their enemies. Mordecai institutes a new Jewish feast, the feast of
purim, to celebrate. The text approves the slaughter without question. It is this feature of the book of Esther which makes the book so
disturbing. Did the writer intend the readers of the book to be
alarmed? Is the writer indicating that this chosen race is no better
than or perhaps even worse than its enemies? Does the writer
intend the reader to marvel at God's solidarity with a people who
show so little mercy? These questions remain unanswered. Perhaps
they suggest too much sophistication in the storyteller, but they are
questions the reader may nevertheless ask in response to the story.
Maybe the book of Esther simply shows the dangerous extremes to
which the idea of being a chosen people can go in disregarding the
rights of those who are not chosen. The topic has a remarkable contemporary relevance.

We have had our doubts about the historical value of the story of
Esther. The same is true of the story of Judith. This book is one of
the seven extra books found in the Greek Septuagint. The original
seems to have been written in Hebrew, but we only have the Greek
translation. The name Judith means 'woman of Judah' or 'Jewess'.

The enemy in the story is 'Nebuchadnezzar who reigned over the Assyrians in the great city of Nineveh' (Judith 1:1). This symbolic most powerful of kings, who rules as head of the most notoriously cruel empire, is in conflict with the symbolic Jewish heroine. History gives way to symbolism as Judith, Nebuchadnezzar and the Assyrians are presented on the same stage. The story is set some time after the return from exile when Nebuchadnezzar was long dead and the Assyrian empire distant history (4:3).

There are two quite distinct parts in the story of Judith. Nebuchadnezzar has supposedly summoned many client nations, Judah among them, to assist him in a campaign against the Medes. At their refusal to come, Nebuchadnezzar sends his general Holofernes to punish them. Bethulia, an imaginary town of Judah, is on the point of surrender to Holofernes. The widow Judith enters the drama in chapter 8. She is described as a very beautiful and God-fearing woman. Judith speaks to two elders of the town and tells them: 'within the days left before you say you will surrender the town to our enemies, the Lord will rescue Israel by my hand' (8:33/8:32). After a lengthy prayer, which recalls that of Esther before facing her ordeal, Judith leaves the town with her maid and is intercepted by Assyrian troops. She offers to provide information for Holofernes' campaign. The scouts are seduced by Judith's beauty and her deception. On arrival at the tent of Holofernes, Judith encourages him not to hesitate in attacking Bethulia, for, she maintains, the people have sinned and God will allow them to be punished. One line of her speech is particularly ironic: 'God has sent me to do with you things at which the whole earth will be amazed' (11:16/11:13). Judith and her maid stay in the Assyrian camp, but are careful to gain permission to go out of the camp in the early morning to pray.

On the fourth day Holofernes holds a banquet and he and his companions summon Judith (Judith 12). At the end of the banquet Judith and Holofernes are left alone, but Holofernes has collapsed on his bed due to drink. Judith uses his scimitar to sever his head, which is reminiscent of Haman's gallows being used to hang Haman. Judith gives the head of Holofernes to her maid, who puts it in her food bag (13:10/13:12). They leave the camp at the hour of prayer, thus causing no alarm. Arriving back in Bethulia Judith displays the head of Holofernes and celebrates her triumph. In the morning the Assyrians discover the headless torso of Holofernes, and they flee, pursued and slaughtered by the Israelites. A canticle of Judith celebrates her mighty deed in the final chapter of the book. It recalls the canticle of Deborah in the book of Judges (Judges 5), and indeed Judith herself reminds the reader of Jael and her killing of the Canaanite army general Sisera (Judges 4). The last line of the book of Judith is similar to the frequent refrain in the book of Judges that after war the people were left in peace: 'Never again during the days of Judith, nor for long after her death, did anyone intimidate the sons of Israel' (16:25/16:30). The books of Esther and Judith show how God strengthens these heroines in time of danger. These books, however, lack the openness to God's care for other nations expressed in more enlightened parts of the Old Testament, such as the poems of Second Isaiah and the book of Jonah.

Tobit and the book of Baruch

From two books memorable for their strong women heroines we can turn to a quieter, domestic tale in the story of Tobit. Like the book of Judith, the book of Tobit is found only in the Greek Bible. As with Judith, the original Hebrew or Aramaic version has been lost. Two stories are interwoven and in both the providence of a caring God is celebrated. It becomes plain early in the book that once again we are dealing with fiction. Tobit maintains that in his youth his tribe of Naphtali broke away from the house of David (Tobit 1:4), a reference to the division of the kingdoms in 921 BC. Tobit also claims he was exiled to Nineveh in the Assyrian period two hundred years later (Tobit 1:3).

Tobit is a man of piety who lives in exile in Nineveh and is zealous in maintaining the law, providing food for the poor and proper burial for his compatriots. The description of his virtue is reminiscent of the description of Job. Resting by the wall of his courtyard one evening, he is blinded when sparrows' droppings fall on his eyes (Tobit 2:10/2:11). Like Job, Tobit is to be tested. He is even reproached by his wife, as Job was, for his tenacious virtue. In the parallel story, Sarah, far away in Media, has lost seven men given to her in marriage, when they were killed one after the other by a demon named Asmodeus. Sarah is reproached in her turn by her servant-girl for killing her seven husbands. The prayer of both Tobit and Sarah is heard by God and Raphael, who later identifies himself as an angel, is sent to their assistance.

Tobit decides to settle his affairs. He gives his son Tobias fatherly advice and sends Tobias to Media to recover some money owed to him. Raphael guides Tobias on the journey to Media. The tale tells how a great fish leaps out of the river Tigris and Raphael instructs the young Tobias to extract its heart, liver and gall. The heart and liver may be burned to frighten away evil demons. The gall is used as an ointment for the eyes.

The reader can already foresee how Raphael, whose name means 'God heals', is providing remedies for both Sarah and Tobit. Raphael reveals that Sarah is related to Tobias and that Tobias has a right to marry her. Tobias already knows that to marry Sarah is to face the danger of a quick death. At Sarah's house her parents welcome Tobias and Raphael but also tell Tobias of the danger he would run in marrying their daughter. While Sarah's father digs another grave, the burning of the fish's heart and liver sends the demon away in flight, pursued by Raphael. The wedding of the two young people is celebrated for two weeks, Tobias sees to his father's business in Media, and bride and bridegroom return home. Needless to say, on their return to Nineveh Tobit is cured of his blindness by application of the fish's gall to his eyes.

To summarise the story of Tobit, Tobias and Sarah is to deprive it of its gentle charm. The story may seem naïve, even childish, but it reveals a deep faith in the providence of God amid the trials of life. It is no accident that the names of both Tobit and Tobias are versions of a Hebrew name which means 'God is good'. The gentle people of the book of Tobit are models for every age, while Raphael is one of three angels named in the Old Testament, the others being Gabriel and Michael in the apocalyptic chapters of Daniel. Late Jewish reflection on how God provides for the people, how secrets are revealed to visionaries, and how the events of the end of the world are to proceed, leads to particular angels being given particular tasks. These angels represent God's care for people and God's mysterious communication in their hearts and minds. Within the story of Tobit there are also some fine prayers, much praise of God, and significant speeches which show similarities to the wisdom tradition. The book is a rich treasury of prayer and teaching.

The book of Baruch is a complex book. Found only in Greek it is placed after the book of Jeremiah and the Lamentations for it bears the name of Jeremiah's scribe. The book shows signs of the post-exilic period and is one of the last books of the Old Testament to be compiled. Baruch is presented as living in exile in Babylon, and reading the book to the deported king Jehoiachin. It contains a fine penitential prayer which shows a deep understanding of sin, a poem in praise of wisdom as a gift of God, words of encouragement to Jerusalem, and a letter condemning idolatry supposedly written by Jeremiah to the exiles.

The last books of wisdom

As we approach the end of the Old Testament period two more books of the wisdom tradition remain to be explored, the book of Sirach (or ben Sira) and the book of the Wisdom of Solomon, well-known simply as the book of Wisdom. Both are preserved in Greek, though original Hebrew texts of Sirach have been discovered in the last one hundred years. The book of Wisdom, it seems, was the only Old Testament book to be written in Greek as the original language of composition.

The story of the completion of the Greek version of the book of ben Sira is a fascinating one. In its Greek translation the book, which is known also as Ecclesiasticus due to its adoption by the church, contains a prologue written by the translator. He reports that his grandfather, Jesus son of Sira, who had long studied the law, the prophets and the other writings, had decided to compile his own collection of teachings. The grandson excuses himself if on occasion his Greek translation has not rendered the Hebrew original adequately. He is aware that the translations of the law, the prophets and the other writings have not always been satisfactory. This is already sufficient indication that he is writing in Egypt, where Greek translations of Hebrew scriptures have been undertaken since the third century BC. The translator confirms this by writing of his arrival in Egypt presumably from Jerusalem and his decision to translate his grandfather's work. This was in the thirty-eighth year of king Euergetes, who was Ptolemy VII, who reigned from 170-117. The work was therefore translated in about 132 BC, and was perhaps written about 180 BC. The book gives personal memories of Simon the high priest, who was in office about 200 BC, and so must have been completed no earlier than his rule (Sirach 50).

For centuries scholars only had the Greek text of the book, but at the end of the nineteenth century a discovery in a manuscript store in an ancient synagogue of Cairo provided texts of Sirach in Hebrew. Subsequent finds at Masada and at Qumran mean that study of the book of ben Sira has been given a new dimension.

The wisdom of ben Sira is a long book of fifty-one chapters. With its aim of providing sound teaching both for Jews and non-Jews, it covers a great variety of topics concerning God, the world and human life. In similar fashion to Proverbs chapter 8, Sirach 24 gives a poem in praise of wisdom, in which personified wisdom speaks. Ben Sira equates wisdom with the law given to Moses (Sirach 24). Both are gifts of God. The Mosaic tradition and the wisdom tradition have fundamentally the same aim of teaching people to live according to God's will. Like the other wisdom books, ben Sira too prizes as the fundamental virtue the 'fear of the Lord', respect and obedience to God's laws. Wisdom brings fear of the Lord, which leads to obedience to the law.

A good example of a topic dear to ben Sira is that of friendship. He warns of accepting a friend too easily, for a faithful friend is a rare treasure. He concludes: 'The one who fears the Lord makes true friendships, for as a person is so will be his fellow' (6:17). While much of ben Sira's teaching has an enduring worth, some of it is conditioned by its time. This is particularly true of his teaching about women. He shares with the book of Proverbs a somewhat condescending view which deserves cautious treatment. His words about banquets, however, seem to have an enduring relevance. The well-bred person is quite content with a limited amount of food and he will sleep better for it (31:19/31:22). Old men have a right to speak, but they should speak with intelligence and not interrupt the music (32:3/32:4-5). Young men, by contrast, should hesitate to speak, keep to the point, and say much in few words (32:7-8/32:9-12).

The final chapters of ben Sira give a survey of the great men of Israel, beginning with Enoch and Noah. The short summaries about patriarchs, prophets and kings show why they were held in esteem by priestly groups in Jerusalem around 200 BC. It seems indeed that ben Sira has a special regard for the members of priestly families and he finishes with a long poem in praise of Simon the high priest. The book of Sirach is filled with precious material, some dated but much of it of lasting use for the reflection of those who attempt to live in the fear of the Lord. As ben Sira declares, there is no possibility of giving God due credit with human words. We can merely confess: 'God is all' (43:27/43:29).

The book of the Wisdom of Solomon is shorter, but just as fascinating. It is not a translation, but written originally in Greek. Like so many books of the wisdom tradition, it is attributed to Solomon, and even has Solomon speak. Found only in the Greek Bible, it seems to have originated in Alexandria some time in the first century BC. Some even claim it was written later than this but a certain influence on the New Testament makes the first century AD the latest possible period of writing. The book is written both to encourage Jews and to attract Gentiles to faith in the God of Israel.

The first five chapters of Wisdom consider the fate of the virtuous and the wicked. The godless see no need for a virtuous life. Death will soon come and with it oblivion. Meanwhile they can oppress the virtuous, whose way of life is a challenge and a reproach to them. The writer affirms that the way of the godless is mistaken, for God has made human beings imperishable (2:23). He explains that it was due to the devil's envy that death entered the world (2:24). This text shows how the story of the expulsion from Eden has been reinterpreted. Though Genesis chapter 3 does not introduce death as a punishment and makes no mention of the devil or Satan, subsequent traditions see death as a consequence of sin and explain sin as due to Satan's envy of human beings once he was expelled from God's presence. The developing faith of Judaism has made Satan the instigator of evil and the tempter of human beings and, with its faith in life after death, considers death to have been introduced by God as punishment for sin.

For the writer of Wisdom the souls (Greek *psychai*) of the virtuous dead are in the hands of God (3:1). This writer does not use the idea of the resurrection of the body to speak of life after death, but the sense of 'soul' is not that of a disembodied spirit. One might translate the text 'the lives of the virtuous are in the hands of God'. The writer affirms the truth of life after death in terms more appropriate to Greek philosophical thinking, but does not propose a detailed explanation of how human beings live beyond death. God will grant life to the virtuous, while for the wicked there will be no future. Wisdom expresses in a different way what Daniel chapter 12 had affirmed in an apocalyptic vision of the resurrection. The catalyst for belief in life after death in Israel was the persecution of Antiochus. God had surely prepared salvation for those who had endured torture and death. The book of Wisdom may well have been written in the wake of the persecution of Jews by the Ptolemies during the second century BC. In chapter 5 the godless are described at their judgement, realising that they were wrong. Their lives have passed without leaving a trace, like a ship cutting the waves, like a bird flying through the air, like an arrow shot at a target (5:10-12). Their hope is vain. The virtuous alone will live.

It is Solomon who speaks in chapter 6-9, though he is never named. Solomon sings the praises of wisdom, which he esteems more than power and riches. The story of Solomon's dream at Gibeon in 1 Kings chapter 3 has inspired these words. Solomon lists twenty-one attributes of the spirit of wisdom, three times seven indicating perfect completeness (7:22-23). A fine prayer of Solomon ends the section in chapter 9. Here too it is clear that the speaker is Solomon the king (9:7).

The final section of the book considers the role of wisdom in history. In chapter 10 several ancient characters are described, but without their names being given. Jacob is the 'virtuous man fleeing from the anger of his brother' (10:10). Wisdom showed him the kingdom of God. Joseph is the 'virtuous man sold but kept free from sin' (10:13). Wisdom accompanied him in prison and brought him the sceptre of a kingdom. Once the writer reaches the time of the exodus there is an extraordinary development. He retells the exodus story from the plagues to the crossing of the sea according to the principle stated in 11:5. God's wisdom uses the same elements to punish Israel's enemies and to save Israel. Waters of blood punish Egypt, while water from the rock saves Israel. A bronze serpent fashioned by Moses saves the Israelites, while locusts and mosquitoes plague the Egyptians. Hail and lightning fall on Egypt, while manna from the heavens delights the people of Israel. It is an intriguing task to identify the different features of the retold story of the exodus in chapters 10-19. God's wisdom is always at work in the people's life. The retelling of the exodus story is particularly apposite for Jews now living among the Egyptians. God cares for the people particularly when like their ancestors they are oppressed by the Egyptians.

There are two digressions in these final chapters. In chapters 13-15 the writer speaks of those who worship idols, even alluding to the worship of animals which was common in Egypt (15:18). Before this he develops the idea of God's forbearance. With both Jews and Gentiles God showed mercy: 'you are merciful to all, because you can do all things, and you overlook the sins of men so that they can repent' (11:23/11:24). The wisdom of the writer describes God as *philopsychos*, which one might translate 'lover of human life' (11:26). God's forbearance is also a lesson for human behaviour. God as lover of human beings (Greek *philanthropos*) teaches how people should behave towards each other (12:19). The author combines his efforts to express the faith of Israel in new language with fidelity to the ancient traditions. His use of Greek ideas to express Old Testament faith is a courageous effort to offer the religious ideas of Israel beyond the confines of Judaism. The Old Testament was destined to follow this path above all in Christian use in the centuries to come.

CHAPTER 14

Alive and active?

This book set out with the clear objective to demonstrate the vitality
and energy of the Old Testament beyond the year 2000. As we
focused on the books and groups of books in the Old Testament
many connections with contemporary situations were suggested. It
is time now to draw some points together. Is it really justified to
claim that these ancient writings are alive and active today?

The search for meaning
There have been throughout history people who have claimed that
life is absurd, that it has no meaning. Those men and women are far
more numerous, however, who have maintained that a meaning
can be discovered in human life and who have been repelled by the
notion that life is absurd. For the Old Testament writers, as for so
many people through the centuries, the search for meaning
involves God. The people of Israel became ever more aware of the
reality of God and of God's effects on their lives as individuals and
as a people. This God of Israel is both close, approachable and
involved, and also distant, inaccessible and aloof. This paradoxical
God is not simply a facile and simplistic answer to the difficult
question of meaning, but the discovery of countless people open to
inspiration and willing to ponder.

The different features of Yahweh, God of Israel, reflect the struggle of people to express in words the meaning they perceive. There
is a developing picture here, but not a complete one. For believers
of past millennia these books revealed the meaning behind life's
facades. For the present and the future, the God of the Old
Testament still rings true for seekers after the meaning of life.

God is understood to be involved with the world and with

human life. The opening chapters of the Old Testament present God as the creator, the originator of the ordered universe, who gave human beings charge of all creatures. The notion emerges that God has a purpose, a benevolent purpose, but a purpose which is somehow hampered by the mysterious evil present in the world. The freedom to choose given by God to human beings has its tragic side. Human beings are free to cross boundaries and to violate their relationship with the creator and with other creatures. Despite the proliferation of evil, this God continues to care for the creation. The God of the patriarchs and matriarchs is above all one who provides, who accompanies and who is faithful. God is considered somehow present in the lives of ordinary people, present in the life of Ruth, who accepts the faith of Naomi, present in the life of Tobit, Tobias and Sarah, who all experience God's providence and healing. The same God is understood as intervening in history in order to liberate a people, to provide them with a land, and to punish their infidelity. This notion of the involvement of God in the history of Israel may seem naïve. Later reflection on God's failure to intervene in human affairs suggested a God who is more distant and more aloof.

This more distant God is present in Genesis chapter 1. The creator described here is not the working God of Genesis chapter 2, but sends out words of command from a distance. The ways of God are far above human ways, as high as the heavens are above the earth. This God is mysterious and teases human beings like Job about how little they can grasp. The God of Solomon cannot be contained in the temple. The God of Elijah is not in earthquake, wind and fire, but mysteriously sensed in a still, small whisper. The God of Isaiah fills the prophet with awe and trembling. The God of Ben Sira is simply 'all'.

The God of the Old Testament is searched for, found and not found. This God can be approached in prayer in good times and bad, a God who hears, a God who responds in the strange ways of God's providing. In shaping their ideas of God the people of the Old Testament used their experiences, individual and communal, they used their prayer, alone or together, and they displayed an extraordinary willingness to listen to other voices. The wisdom of the nations is listened to and sometimes adopted. These people searched for meaning by listening, listening to life, listening for the signs of meaning and the signs of God. Their search for meaning is ours too.

The search for justice

This benevolent God, who remains well-disposed to human beings despite their abuse of freedom, must surely desire justice for people. The providing God of Genesis is also the liberating God of Exodus. In fact it seems that experience of God's liberation in their lives led them to grasp that God was also creator of all. God wants the good of the people, their freedom and well-being. This powerful image of God has repeatedly inspired believers to work for the good of all, has constantly given courage to the oppressed and has consistently raised up people who work to break unjust fetters and to fight for freedom and equality. The God of liberation is as potent an inspiration today as in the days of the prophets.

The God of Moses wants people to live in freedom and in mutual love. Laws and customs by which Israel's life was to be guided are seen as gifts of the God of Moses. God who brought Israel out of Egypt required Israel to live by these laws. The resistance human beings demonstrate in following God's ways is seen as another feature of the mysterious evil in the world. As centuries went by, new laws were drafted as laws of Moses, laws derived from the Sinai covenant. God is bound to the people and they are bound to God. God gives them the laws of life. The just God requires the people to do justice, to love fidelity and to go humbly with their God. Their response is mixed.

The God of Moses is the God of the prophets, those who speak out for justice when men and women oppress their fellows. The prophets of Israel teach that people should work for justice and peace in and for the present, not for some remote future. The prophets have a passion for present justice, for present peace, and for the necessary conversion of heart. Their hope is for a kingdom where justice and peace reign. They speak in God's name to challenge unjust structures, evil actions and lack of hope. They trust in the all-embracing providence of God despite the constant failures to live according to God's laws.

As time progresses there is a growing awareness of God as the God of all peoples. All nations are cherished, even Assyria and Babylon. All nations are to live in the knowledge of the one, true God. Though the nation of Israel is understood as having a particular role in history as the witness of the one God, Israel realises that all nations are equally loved and cared for. This opening to the nations is somewhat uncertain, for each individual believer must make the same journey from suspicion and fear to openness and acceptance.

The search for justice calls for an answer to the question of the meaning of suffering. Israel realises that the simplistic traditional answers are deficient. When a nation is tormented, serious questions about God's justice are raised. When a good person suffers, there seems to be no justice. Yahweh's words to Job suggest a broader scenario, a world where the freedom God gives to all creatures means that evil cannot be immediately dispensed with, that pain cannot be immediately cured, that the anguish of peoples and nations is part of the mystery. The fourth poem of the servant suggests a new dimension to innocent suffering, but the inspired writers of the Old Testament can only put in writing what human language can express and what the human mind can fathom. There are more things in heaven and earth than can be explained in human theologies.

The search for peace
The God of the Old Testament is understood as creating all in harmony, a harmony which is undermined by *ra'*, evil, all that is not good. The *shalom* which God desires, the state of everything being at ease, is lost. But God continues to care, providing for that *shalom*. The catastrophe of the flood is not God's final word to creation. The rainbow is a sign of solidarity with all creatures. The catastrophe of the destruction of Jerusalem is not God's final word to Israel. The exile and the return display God's enduring care. After disaster comes a new beginning. God provides for people to live in peace.

The individual seeks peace in the prayers of so many psalms. Peace comes from forgiveness of sin, from deliverance from enemies or natural disaster, from trustful security guaranteed by a caring God. The prayer can be for the peace of the nation, for the peace of Jerusalem, for the peace of the world. The reassurance given to Jeremiah in his turmoil, the courage given to Esther and to Judith, speak too of God's *shalom*.

Prophets have visions of peace among the nations. The nations will come to learn the laws of God. Foreigners will take Jews by the sleeve and ask to be led to the holy city of God. Nations will stream to the light of Sion. Swords will be made into ploughshares and spears into pruning hooks. The weapons of war will be burnt. There will be no more need for armaments. There will be no more fear. The vision of international peace seen by the prophets is a powerful and enduring one. They still proclaim it as God's will for the people of the earth.

Peace needs foundations of justice, of acceptance and mutual respect. The Old Testament reflects the struggle of the nation and of individuals to turn from fear to courage, from prejudice to openness, from suspicion to love. The task to build a world in accordance with the creator's will remains today. The book of Daniel speaks of a kingdom to be established by God. There is an enduring hope that God's will will be done, that God's kingdom will come. Human beings meanwhile strive that this may be so. God's way is to use human beings with their precious freedom to love or not love in the building of the kingdom.

The search for a future

The fact of death cries out to human beings that life is absurd, that life is meaningless. Israel's experience of God as creator, provider and liberator suggested that God's care is not brought to an end by death. The God who brought all things into being from chaos and who placed man and woman at the peak of creation surely had both the power and the will to preserve them beyond death. The nation grew in faith as it understood that God provides a future for people beyond death. God's faithful would be taken to God like Moses and

Elijah. This future life is shrouded in mystery but it is presented as a vindication of the faithful, and as a reward for those who strove to live in God's life-giving ways.

Critical times of persecution and martyrdom revealed the truth of life beyond pain and beyond death. God's justice required vindication of God's holy ones. Life must be offered to such as these, though the features of such life were impossible for human beings to fathom. God, the book of Wisdom proclaims, is *philopsychos*, 'lover of human life'. Such a God would not bring all to nothingness in death.

A search which first discovered God as liberator understood this God also as creator and provider. This benevolent and powerful God must finally have sway over death as over life. This God provides for human beings throughout life, throughout history, beyond life, beyond history. Israel's faith had faced the mystery of death.

Beyond 2000

The Old Testament shows how the people of Israel searched for truth and searched for answers. Through listening for God in their lives they became more deeply aware of God's mystery. New insights of God were received over centuries and preserved from generation to generation by the community. Each new believer learnt from these insights and built on them. Some ideas had to be dropped, though some were stubbornly persistent. But the journey continued, the journey of a people and the journeys of individuals towards the truth of God.

The journey of God's people is not finished. For Christians the books of the Old Testament are complemented by those of the New Testament, the books concerned with Jesus, his life and death, his resurrection and the meaning of all these. Christians need the Old Testament to assist their understanding of Jesus the Jew, and they can learn from the journey of Israel for their own journey to God. For those too who are not Christians, the Old Testament is a valuable gift because it courageously faces life's questions and provides an enduring revelation which helps each person journey towards truth.

For Christian and non-Christian alike, the search for meaning and the quest for peace and justice continue, as history continues. There is always more to understand, more to perceive. A deeper awareness beckons. I offer this book to Christians, that it may enliven their faith in the Jesus who came to bring the law and the prophets to fulfilment. Indeed, I offer it to all who seek meaning and truth in their lives beyond 2000.

Suggested further reading

B. Anderson, *The Living World of the Old Testament*, Longman
This classic introduction to the literature of the Old Testament by an American Old Testament scholar is illustrated with copious pictures and maps, and has reached its fourth edition.

L. Boadt, *Reading the Old Testament. An Introduction*, New York: Paulist Press
Laurence Boadt offers a full and attractively presented treatment of the literature.

A. Ceresko, *Introduction to the Old Testament. A Liberation Perspective*, London: Chapman
A full introduction to the books of the Old Testament with particular emphasis on their social relevance

H. Jagersma, *A History of Israel to Bar Kochba*, London: SCM Press
This Dutch scholar provides a very clear account of the history of Israel in Old Testament and New Testament times.

V. Matthews & D. Benjamin, *Old Testament Parallels*, New York: Paulist Press
Matthews and Benjamin provide translations of many of the writings from the nations surrounding Israel which have connections with biblical books.

R. E. Murphy, *Responses to 101 Questions on the Biblical Torah*, New York: Paulist Press
A user-friendly way of presenting the conclusions of scholarship on the Pentateuch.

R. E. Murphy, *Responses to 101 Questions on the Psalms and Other Writings*, New York: Paulist Press
An attractive approach to some of the lesser known writings.

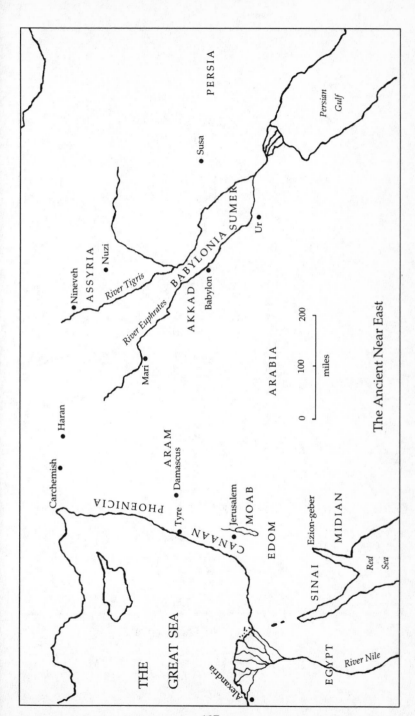

The Ancient Near East

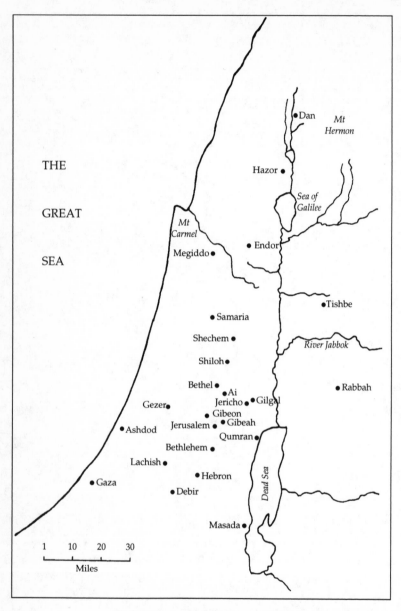

THE

GREAT

SEA

Mt Hermon

●Dan

Hazor ●

Sea of Galilee

Mt Carmel

Megiddo ●

● Endor

● Tishbe

● Samaria

River Jabbok

Shechem ●

Shiloh ●

Bethel ● ● Ai

● Rabbah

Jericho ● ● Gilgal

Gezer ●

Gibeon ●

Jerusalem ● ● Gibeah

Ashdod ●

Qumran ●

Bethlehem ●

Dead Sea

Lachish ●

● Gaza

● Hebron

● Debir

Masada ●

1   10   20   30

Miles

Palestine in Old Testament Times

188

Index of biblical books and biblical people